My Newest Boc

The sequel to My Sequel-Innit?

(The sequel to My Book-Innit?)

Wayne Reid
(The Sequel to Ribsy-Innit?)

DEDICATION

To my beautiful wife Laurel Reid, for all you have done, and all that you do, there are not enough "Thank You's".

In Loving Memory Of my Father Ernie John Reid x

And Linda Hayes x

"You can't put your arms around a memory…" Johnny Thunders

CONTENTS

DISCLAIMER

The contents of this book, it's story, characters, names and places are all fictional and do not relate to anyone alive, dead, or yet to be born. It's not about you, never was, never will be

1 Kings Of The Wild Frontier

Epitaph

I sit here in my silence and look up at the stars, then back upon my history "My God! I went too far."

There was nothing there to stop me, there were no barriers then, now it is too late to change, it is as it was then.

Young and free- so foolish, but clever enough to smile, wise enough to miss you while sad enough to cry.

Full of preservation but myself I left behind, to give all to some other folk who in turn kept up with time.

Now they pass before me, they smile and say "Hello!"

I say "I'm doing well now" though I haven't long to go.

I smell it on the inside-the outside stays intact, but the rot's so deep it hides itself, too well within the cracks.

Until my darkest hour, my life shall be fulfilled, passing pleasures unto others and their strength I hope to build.

I thank you for the times we've shared as I look up to the stars, beside me pass the healthy, the wealthy drive in cars.

You know that we're all born to die, and I wish you could have cared, now all I have is passed in time with the memories that we shared......

I never asked to be born, I had no interest in it really. I was happy in my ignorance, warm and dark, devoid of all external influence. I didn't care what lay beyond the dark void I inhabited, I heard no sound, saw no colour, felt no pain. There was only myself, an eternity of nothing around me, and that was all I needed. All I needed to be free and content in my own vacuum of space. Somebody else had other ideas though. Somebody else decided that I was needed, I had a purpose, a job to do, a place and time to be, and that place and time was now, in what I can only describe as a real fuck up of human mismanagement. I was pulled, kicking and screaming from the womb, no warnings, no preparation, no training. All I could do was breathe and just as I did so, some bitch slapped me on the arse so hard all I could do was scream. I'd never felt anything before, hugs, cuddles, soft blankets, a dog's wet tongue tasting my face, nothing. I was not prepared, but by Christ I was mightily pissed off. Those first moments of my life set the tone for what was to come, retribution. I was never again going to be knocked down and unable to fight back, I would always stand up for myself, fight back until all the fight was gone. I was never going to give in, unless of course, there was ice cream to be had.

Growing up was a long slog, but at the end, there was a payback. Freedom and the open road, there was alcohol, music and sex. Growing up was going to be good fun, hell, it was going to be the best of times, sitting in a shitty nappy wasn't my idea of fun, I wanted more, I wanted what the big people had- fun. I wanted to shed that diaper and pee straight onto the carpet, I wanted to stand up and fart in a way that would make my folks proud of me.

"Mum, listen to this!"

Paaaaaarpp!

It's all a little boy wants really, recognition for having created something all by himself. To know his elders notice his presence, even if it is by sense of smell. Little boys make noise, they smell and if left alone for too long, they'll burn the bloody house down. It's what we do, what we are programmed for and what some specialise in.

Growing up meant bigger toys, brighter lights and getting around faster. It meant swapping my skateboard for a bike, and then a car. The world was my oyster, I could come and go as I pleased, and frequently did. I could drive anywhere I wanted, whenever I wanted, I was free, all I needed was a bit of petrol money and an idea. I didn't need food, shelter, none of the things that tie you down to one place. I needed nothing I couldn't carry with me. I roamed wild and free for years, doing mostly as I pleased until doing as I pleased lost its appeal. All about me, good friends were settling down, the next generation of their bloodline stewed away in the bellies of loved ones, boiling, growing bigger by the moment, stretching and pushing at the thin skin of their mother's womb, scratching to find what lay outside. That was me once, in there looking out, wondering what the fuck was going on and why I wasn't invited, why I was alone. That feeling stuck with me forever, I was always alone, even when I was in a crowd, I was alone, because nobody really knew me, nobody felt what I felt, nobody was me other than myself, and I wasn't sure that I was ever good enough for me.

I tried to settle down, I really did. I gave up everything for love, again and again. Each time it soured I tried again, I never gave up until the day I did give up, and that hurt, deep inside it hurt and I knew I had to go away again.

No matter what I made, no matter what I created, I had to leave. The pain of failure, the hopeless desperation of once more getting it wrong left me no choice. Outside the wind called me, it hummed quietly along the surface of the tarmac, rippling above oily pools of spilled diesel until it filled my nostrils once again with it's sweet free aroma, the enticing scent of adventure, big horizons and wide open seas. How could I resist her calling, how could I not answer when I'd been silent for too long? My world had turned to shit again, and it was time to move on.

Eilat was a long way behind me. A faint memory buried deep in the vaults of my mind, but at the same time a constant companion. Nothing would ever be the same, nothing could ever beat the thrill of riding those storms, rocking and rolling in the maelstrom of a howling gale, spinning like a toy in mid air as the sea rose and fell, pulled to the very limit of human endurance as I clung desperately between the Israeli Navy Buoy and the bowline of a 200 ton ship. I was the weakest link, in my yellow shorts with their cigarette burn in the backside, I was the weakest link, and yet all those lives aboard depended on me, me and my dirty yellow shorts with the cigarette hole in the backside. I did that whilst riding a camel, you know, trying to smoke when lumbering along on a camel's back in the full heat of the desert sun, not expecting a sudden jolt, dropping the cigarette and promptly sitting on it not knowing where it had fallen. I soon found out though, I soon knew where it was.

The memory of that foray into the Middle East seared my mind daily, not because I regretted coming back, not because I had failed as a father to my son, but because it was there, like the greatest victory I'd ever achieved, the one story I had to tell again and again, to relive, again and again, on a daily fucking basis, again and again, it was there, it was part of me, part of who I am, and I could not get rid of it any more than I could get rid of that smile, the one that twists the corners of my mouth up every time I fart. I could not get rid of Eilat, not unless I could find another high, another adventure or cause that would lead me astray to some far corner of the world.

Looking for adventures is easy, we all do it, the hard part is recognising them when they arrive, seeing the opportunity before it floats by on it's ethereal way out the door and into the path of the next willing risk taker. Adventures are all around, they can be plucked from the air easily once you are tuned to their frequency. A simple job advertisement, a conversation with a friend, someone you've just met or a planned event. All can lead to adventures. I am often asked what I do in the 'real' world, the answer is simple really, in that real world I do the same as everyone else, I work for a living, I sell my soul for a wage, prostituting my body for the currency of the day, giving up my freedoms for 'The Man', that faceless, soulless, corporate identity that sends chicken feed to my bank each week, so that I can enrich and empower those in their Ivory towers. You could say that, or you could say, I work for a living, I am a worker, the lifeblood of the land. I tend to stick with the easier to understand label of being a 'Truck Driver'. People understand that. They picture my fat arse spreading across the cushion of a seat in a greasy spoon cafe, hairy arms dangling from the window of a cab desperately seeking a one sided suntan, the near side is always in the shade, inside the cab, pale and skinny, the right arm tanned and muscled from lots of sunshine and week after week masturbating across the European road network, it's a lonely night when the engine goes off and there's nobody to talk to.

Being a truck driver has always provided me with adventures though, and if you stop checking the muscles on my right arm, I may just tell you about some of them.

The idea of being a truck driver never appealed to me, never. It was only after having lived in France and returning to England -after a few months in Los Angeles, that I started to think about ways of getting the hell out of Dodge- the UK was not where I wanted to be, I wanted out, out there, somewhere, anywhere but here. My options were limited, sparse actually if not not downright bloody non-existent. I had no money, no trade, no skills or means by which to seek a career beyond the white cliffs.

I began working in a steel drum refurbishing plant in East London, my income was minimum wage before they'd even coined the phrase. I worked hard, smelled bad and drank too much beer to ever get my life straight. What I did have, was hope, and a desire to do better. I also had a conversation with a couple of hairy armed truckers, busy eating bacon rolls, or were they cobs? Maybe Batches? Barmcakes? Possibly Butties?

"How much do you get a week?" I didn't beat about the bush, I wanted to know how much they got paid to eat bacon and drink tea while the rest of us sweated our little nuts off.

"If I do a couple of nights out, Liverpool or South Wales" *swallows a mouthful of tea,* "I get £180 a week, otherwise just about £140 for a flat week".

I was gutted, that was twice what I was earning, and I wasn't eating bacon, at least, not 3 times a day. I wanted some of this action, I wanted to go to Wales and Liverpool, I wanted to get lots of money so I could go back to Delaware and reclaim my girlfriend, Marybeth. I'd fallen foul of her father and left her behind whilst I sorted myself out in the UK, something I never got round to doing, not for a long time. I wanted to travel the world across deserts and mountains, eat weird food and do crazy stuff, things I'd never been told were possible by my career adviser at school. Those people knew nothing of the outside world, seriously. If all you can advise kids to aspire to is an 8 hour shift in a factory and are scared shitless of a life on the dole, then you need to up your game. You need to rethink your options and possibilities. There is, as I found, a whole world out there waiting for you to discover, and discover you should in any and every way you can.

My gateway to the big wide world was through this simple conversation, a realisation that I could earn more money by sitting on my arse and looking out the window. How hard could that be? I love a good cup of tea and can rarely say no to a bacon-whatever-it-is, sandwich, barm cake, bap, batch.....

So there I was, sitting in the seat of the biggest machine I'd ever controlled, trying my best to control the biggest machine I'd ever sat in. I didn't remember the trucks my Dad had driven ever feeling so big. Even as a nipper heading off up the motorway to Sheffield, Wales or Germany, I never felt the trucks to be so huge. Maybe I never thought about it, maybe it didn't matter, or maybe it was just sitting in the driving seat gave a whole new perspective, whatever it was, I suddenly felt less in control and more at the mercy of this great lumbering beast.

"For fuck's sake, have a word with yourself man. You passed your test, you come from truck driving stock, you've got this, come on, you can do it!" I sucked in some cold, early morning air, the taste of exhaust fumes so thick I felt like I'd eaten a second breakfast. This was my first day out alone. Just me, a Leyland Marathon pulling a 40ft long tandem axle flatbed trailer. My training may have ended, the test passed, but the real learning was just about to start.

It doesn't matter how well you do in your test, how easy you find the training, the real learning starts when you're out there, doing it. Your elders become your reference tool, their knowledge and experience become your back-up plan, you learn from those that have been there and done it, those who know where you're going, what you're yet to see. You listen, you learn, you observe and you take it all in, filtering out the bullshit as you go.

I put the truck in gear, a process involving having to press down on the clutch pedal with all my might, my left foot feeling the full resistance of 32 tons of heavy steel not wishing to cooperate, my left knee trembling against the pressure, as I poetically stirred the gear stick in a vain attempt to seek a gear position somewhere in this worn out box of porridge. As I released the clutch there was no response, nothing, I'd failed to find a gear, pushed back down again on the pedal, stirred again and felt something vibrating through the bones of my left arm, followed by a click and I was in, I lifted the pedal again and the truck moved slowly forward.

"Fuuuuuuuuuuuccccck!" I had this, I was in control and nothing could stop me now, diesel pumped through my veins as day after day I learned and perfected my craft, working ever onward toward my ultimate goal of having a truck of my own, heading off beyond the horizon.

My first Job lasted a couple of months, I learned the basics, getting from A to B without hitting anything in between, without losing anything from the load, except the occasional tray or two of beer that may or may not have found its way into the trailers storage box. As the residents of the Scottish town of Lockerbie ran in search of survivors from the Pan Am airplane wreckage strewn around their town, I loaded my car with trays of beer borrowed from the day's load, headed home and invited my mates round to share in my good fortune.

My next job took me to Spain several times. Thumping up and down national roads to avoid paying the motorway tolls, but still trying to turn my £300 trip money into a decent weekly wage, working day and night to squeeze a 10 day trip into 6, without getting arrested, fined or dead on the tarmac. After this, I progressed through a series of different jobs, Europe was my stomping ground, I'd happily head to Austria with the same outlook as most of my friends going from Coventry to Nottingham. Distance was no barrier, it was a challenge, something to adjust to but never fear.

I was never scared of being away from home, alone in the back end of beyond at night was no different to being alone in bed at home, loneliness is loneliness, homesick is sick of being home, I wanted to be away and enjoyed being anywhere, especially if it meant me being somewhere I'd never been before, discovery (by myself) was the name of the game, seeing things I'd never seen before. I was having a ball, a real-life adventure, mountains, sea crossings, exotic foods, people and places I'd never otherwise get to see, lakes, beaches, forests, restaurants and bars by the dozen. I was being paid to get drunk all over Europe, or at least, that was my interpretation of the agreement between myself and my employers. So long as I got the goods to the consignee, whatever I did in my own free time was my concern. My job was to get there and back in one piece, and for the most part, I did just that.

There were times when things did go a little awry. Like the time I collected 13 helicopter engines from a warehouse in Feltham, West London.

"You've got a million pound's worth of engines there, don't roll it" said my boss when he gave me the details. A million pounds, what I could do with a million pounds, not that I'd ever have it, but it did make me think. It wasn't until I loaded up, strapped the load and headed off to Dover that things started to get stranger. I was headed for Biarritz in Southwest France, to a military base where the engines were due to be serviced. At Dover I was presented with 13 T-Forms, each with a statistical value of £1,000,000. My boss, Peter Howard, had not been given the full picture.

"How much Goods in Transit do we have?" I asked when I called him.

"£250,000, why?"

"I've got £13,000,000 on board now"

"Well you'd better not roll it then."

And that was all the advice I'd ever get. It didn't matter what was on my trailer, I was not to roll the truck. I kept to my end of the deal, I stayed upright and no matter what was thrown at me, I got the job done. In this instance, I did what all good drivers did when they blew a tyre near Paris, I pulled into a garage and replaced it with the spare wheel. This took a couple of hours and ate into my sleep time. I pulled over when my time was up and wound my clock forward, by doing this I could still be at Biarritz for 0800, so long as I wasn't caught by the police on route.

I got on my bunk around 10pm setting my alarm for 0200, it was a short night, but I'd manage, I was 5 hours away from the delivery which meant I could stop for a break on the way down, a quick coffee, 20 minute cat nap, all would be well, and was. Until.....0150 I was rudely awoken by what I thought was an earthquake. My truck had suddenly shaken and I rolled off the bunk, dazed and confused, I shook the sleep from my eyes and became aware of a red light outside, if it was a Hooker she was really working.

"What the....?"

The red light turned white, came towards and then crashed into the front bumper of my old ERF E14, or Plastic Pig as we referred to it on account of the plastic cab within which I was now, once more, laying. My first thought was Aliens, I was being attacked by Aliens, on a motorway service area in France. It seemed to make sense to me at the time, I mean, probin' time, we've all been there, right?

The white light went out and the red returned, I pulled my curtain open enough to see the back end of a Mercedes car disappear behind the bright white lights of it's reverse warning system, another crash and I was once again on my knees on the engine cover between the seats.

"Fuckin' aliens, I'll 'ave you, you bastards!" I jumped into the driver's seat, turned the engine and my headlights on before pulling back the curtains, because nothing scares Aliens more than the sight of a human being in crusty Y-fronts, especially when he's in the driving seat of a 38 ton "Plastic Pig".

The Mercedes burned rubber and shot off the truck parking lot, the sight of my crusty's through it's blacked out windows, obviously being enough to win the day. I sat there momentarily, trying to take in what had just happened when my alarm went off, I bolted upright and promptly added another layer of crust to my underpants.

"Fuckin' aliens!" I was not a happy bunny.

My first time in old East Germany was also an eye opener. I was destined for Berlin and once I crossed the now invisible, defunct border, it was like entering a different time zone, about 50 years backwards. It was almost impossible to speed as the motorway, or Autobahn, was built of cobblestones, not concrete and tarmac. The truck bounced and rocked, shook itself to within an inch of it's terminal breath, the Rictus Grin on my face fixed permanently as my teeth were now melded, the heat generated by my fillings rubbing together and solidifying when I stopped to refuel with cheap diesel. The pump itself, gushed with all the power and pressure of a dehydrated 80 year old with gallstones, pissing into a head wind. My next challenge was to find a phone to call home. I finally managed to find one in Dresden 3 days later and the wife wasn't too impressed.

"What, they haven't got public phone boxes in East Germany?" She demanded

"None that work, no."

Impracticalities aside, travelling around Europe meant sampling lots of local fayre. Food, beer, wine and anything else that I'd never come across in the UK. In Spain I discovered Tortilla's, bocadillo's and Bacardi, lots and lots of Bacardi. There were no measures, just pour it into a tall glass and add a splash of cola to colour it. So very civilised, until the morning after, which, in Spain, is usually about 3 hours later as nobody goes out anywhere until about midnight when the air is cooler and the Brits are comatose on the beach. But the greatest thing to come out of Spain, other than the very cheap bottles of Jack Daniels Gold Medal Replicas from La Jonquera, had to be Cafe Con Leche, coffee with milk. Now you may not like white coffee, you may not like coffee at all, or tea, but there's something about Cafe Con Leche in Spain that makes it the best hot drink you'll ever drink anywhere in the sun. Some say it's because they use sterilised milk, I don't know, or care, I just love it, and I'm a black coffee drinker.

In Germany I was introduced to Currywurst Mit Pommes Frites, that's curried sausage with chips for the uninitiated. In Holland, hot Peanut butter sauce to have with Chicken, Blue Steaks and Croissants in France whilst in Hungary I was given a breakfast of Turkish coffee (complete with grains in the cup) thick brown bread and a generous portion of lard. I did wonder if I was being tested, but the locals were all eating it and so I tucked in too.

Coming home from Sicily once, I stopped in a service area to grab a drink and a snack. I got a bottle of soda, probably a fanta, I was big on that at the time, having just read Ffyona Campbell's book about walking the length of Africa and always being able to find Fanta even when there was no water. At the counter I saw what looked like a soft roll with ham and a big dollop of creme fresh.

"Perfect, I'll have one of those" I said pointing at the batch, barm cake, cob thingy on the counter. I parted with about a telephone number's worth of Lire and headed back out into the sun. Once on the road I took a bite and expecting the creme to squidge out the sides, I took just a little nibble. Instead of spreading around my cheeks, the contents stayed firm and the surprising texture made me jolt, spitting out the mouthful I'd already taken in. What I thought to be a huge dollop of creme was actually some bright white meat I'd never come across before. My meal was ruined, the expectation now destroyed by the fact. I was gutted and unable to eat the rest of it.

A later visit to Sicily left me stranded in the port at Palermo. I was desperate for an ice cream and wandered up the street, to the opera house and beyond, down side streets and back ,eventually returning to the port. On an island where the locals eat on average 8 ice creams a day, I couldn't find one single gelateria, none. No matter where I went, who I asked, nobody wanted to sell me an ice cream, it was as though I was just not Sicilian enough to be allowed an ice cream on a hot summer evening.

Truck driving around Europe can itself be a great adventure. One never knows when the roads in France will be blockaded, or when the Spanish will go on strike, run out of electricity, or just not turn up today, or tomorrow either. When the French farmers shut the roads and ports down in the early 1990's, I was on my way to Paris and got the news before leaving home. Knowing the A26 was shut at the St Omer péage, the port of Calais was besieged as always -as was Boulogne, I caught a ferry to Dunkerque and once off the ferry, pulled over to let everyone else race off into the blockades. Once the last truck off passed me, I slowly pulled away and headed out of the dock. I did this so that whatever was in front of me, I could be pretty sure nothing was behind and I could reverse my way back out of any situation that lay ahead. I drove to the Autoroute and could see the queue of stopped vehicles. I diverted away towards the town of St Omer, entering the town was another blockade, it reached back beyond a roundabout but from where I was, I could see that the road out of St Omer was clear. There was no traffic coming, so I crossed lanes, drove the wrong way around the roundabout and passed the blockade. A cheer went up inside my head and I drove on ignoring the shouts from the protesters on the island. Further along another roadblock had been made by two trucks parking nose to nose across a junction. I estimated from afar there was probably enough room to get through, if I was wrong I might just lose a wing or a mirror. I gunned the engine and headed downhill at the gap, a couple of drivers had placed themselves between the trucks but dived out of my way as I got too close, their nerve broke before mine and with inch perfect, precision driving ('cause I'm good like that!), I got through the gap and left another group of protesters in my rear view mirrors. Lady Luck had definitely been shining on me and as I pulled out of St Omer I headed across the country and down the N1 to Paris. I'd managed to avoid all the roadblocks, even when I was sent across to Eastern France for my reload, I managed to get back via Luxembourg without any delays.

For every trip that went well, there were plenty that didn't. For 6 whole weeks I drove around Europe under a rain cloud, literally. When I was home it was raining, I left for Germany and was followed by a big wet cloud that drained it's contents on me all day, and all night. It followed me home and then down to Paris, across to Eastern France, Belgium, Luxembourg. It followed me to Austria, Italy and Spain. For 6 whole weeks the pitter-patter of droplets hitting the truck's roof would keep me in a state of semi-consciousness at night, not quite awake, but definitely not sleeping. The grey sky seemed to hold an endless supply of cloud and rain and I wondered if I had entered some new state of permanence, slightly damp on the outside and pretty damn miserable inside. Everywhere I went, it rained, but when I called home the sun was shining and everyone was having a lovely time outside, everyone but me. I found myself getting ever more depressed, at least Noah had an Ark, I had a bloody truck, that was never going to float off to some Utopian future, it was going to sink with me inside, licking the windows.

There were times when being away was the best thing ever, the Sun would shine, the deep blue skies kissed the tops of the Alps or shimmered down over the dry desert-like wilds of rural Spain. In Italy, I would take every opportunity to brown my skin in the sun whilst thinking back to my youth, remembering a family holiday to Lido Di Jesolo, where , as a kid, I discovered watermelon for the very first time. I gorged myself on the wet flesh inside these huge green balls. Spitting out the pips was a great new game, it felt rebellious and refreshing. We'd walk along the beach in the afternoon, the sand so hot as to burn the soles of our lily white feet, whilst navigating through the rows of dark brown and blistering bodies laid out around us. I remember a young child being run over outside our hotel, much like Joanne, my younger sister would be in later years, crossing the road outside our house. Most of all, I remembered the wonderful spaghetti and pasta dishes we'd eat, I didn't know what Parmesan cheese was, I'd never experienced it until this holiday, so when I saw the spiky little shavings, I thought they were part of the pasta, and back at school after the holidays argued adamantly that Italians ate spiky spaghetti. On our return, we travelled by train and were treated to an ice cream at Milan railway station. When I demanded a 2nd it was refused, so I spent the whole of the return journey crying and sulking in my bed in the sleeper cabin we had to bring us through the Alps and back home.

Every trip to Italy, I would remember those times, just as each visit to Belgium reminded me of our holiday in Oostende, the smell of the sea and fresh fish forever ingrained in my memory.

In Germany, I would remember driving along with my Dad on the autobahn, looking at the convoys of military vehicles we'd pass, and the sense of disappointment that the soldiers wore green khaki, instead of the blue-grey uniforms of the hundreds of plastic German soldiers I played with for hours on end on the living room floor at home. I would also remember the characters from the Sven Hassel books I'd read as a youngster, Tiny Tim, Porta, Little John. Where were they now, had they survived the war, then what became of them, how had they transitioned from their survival in every hell-hole of the Second World War, to this new Europe and these freedoms we now take so much for granted?

Europe had become my playground, I knew my way around like a local. I could speak French, knew enough German, Italian and Spanish to always manage most situations. I'd worked out that whatever I was doing, I had to imagine I was back home, doing the same. If I went into an office, delivering a load, it would be the same conversation everywhere.

"Hello, I am delivering this to you!" Is the same as;
"Bonjour, j'ai une livraison pour vous!" or maybe
"Guten tag. Ich habe dich......"

Stop sniggering at the back there......

Communication is very important wherever you are and whatever you're doing. The one thing guaranteed to irritate me is some jumped up ignoramus telling me "You can't do that!"

"You can't put that there!"

Well,I beg to differ, because if I can't do it, how come I already have? How is it that I have achieved the impossible task you are reprimanding me for? Don't be telling me what I can't do, tell me what I should be doing, then and only then, will I pay you any attention or respect.

Another one too often heard is- "We've had bigger than that in here!" This is usually followed by the sound of "Oops!" and folding metal.

I was on my way to Marseille once, having collected a machine of sorts, from a factory in Yorkshire. It was actually a control panel, part of an oil rig that BP were building in Southern France. I'd asked which way I was to go as the tallest part was higher than the roof of my trailer.

"Take any route you like, just get it there in one piece. Everyday it's not on site once it's needed, there'll be a cost of £125,000 So no accidents, you can get there any way you want, but it needs to be there in 2 weeks time or else."

I had no intention of taking two weeks, I wanted to be home by the weekend, but that was never going to happen, so I popped in on my way down to Dover. I would always stop by if I could, say hello to the wife and kids, make sure they don't forget me.

"Hi, remember me? We met at the Registry Office, what's for dinner?"

I left early in the morning and got to Dover around 0800, cleared customs and headed to the booking office. All was going ever so well and I was duly booked on the next ferry.

"You'll have to put me on the top deck though," I said before the young lady could finish the booking details, "the load is quite high!"

"How high is it?"

"About 4.5 metres I guess, I haven't measured it, but the trailer is 4 metres tall and I reckon it stands about half a metre above the roof line ." I had passed the ball into her court, it was her fault now, whatever happens.

"You'll be fine, we have 5 metre clearance on the bottom deck." I wasn't convinced, so when I was called forward to board, I called the crew over to keep an eye on my trailer. I slowly inched forward and rose up on the link-span, this was fine because if the front goes up, the rear leans back and just at the right moment I entered the hull of the ferry and levelled off, slowly advanced and parked. Climbing up between the back of my cab and trailer, I could now see that there was about a cigarette width gap between the top of the load and the ceiling. This was not good, because getting off at Calais meant going down the link-span and raising the back as it does so. I could lower the suspension on the trailer, that would give me a bit of extra space but probably not enough still.

"Faites attention á la haut!" *("Watch the top!")* I commanded a crewman as he urged me forward to disembark. I edged forward until my front axle mounted the linkspan and the cry went out.

"Arrete! Arrete!" Accompanied by the inevitable waving of arms. I was stuck, wedged between the link span and the upper deck, there was no way out. The rest of the passengers disembarked freely around me, every car seemed to crawl by, their occupants looking at me in bewilderment, as if I had willingly obstructed their exit.

The ship's crew eventually approached me and as we stood there surveying the options, more and more arrived, the Chief Loading Officer was talking into his radio.

"Oui, Oui, Oui, c'est vachement grave, he cannot exit ze sheep!" It sounded like we were having Mutton for dinner. "Ze Capitaine is coming." Ideas were thrown around, should we move it this way a few feet? Should we turn it around and reverse off? How about letting all the tyres down. As far as I was concerned, "We" did not include me.

"There's only one way of getting this off here, and that's by going back to Dover, reversing off and reloading onto the upper deck." The upper deck being where I had originally asked to be loaded, it was preferable as it was an open deck and therefore nothing to get wedged under.

The ship's captain arrived and the conversation rattled on without me. Arms waved, voices rose and fingers pointed. They would not listen to my idea, so I left them to it. Beyond the link span I could see row upon row of cars, vans and trucks, fired up ready to board. Their driver's anxious to get on and head for the restaurants, duty free and bars. Wives dragged furiously on cigarettes as little Jonathan, in the back, sat cross legged, crying for the toilet and another Bonbon. They knew something was wrong, and that something had something to do with me, it was my fault, I was holding everyone up, they should have been upstairs by now, eating, drinking and letting the kids out of the car, free to run wild around the passenger decks. I could feel the tension rising as engines revved and people stared accusingly.

"Monsieur, we will try to wemove ze air from your tyres and zen you can drive off, no?"

"No pal, if I let the tyres down how do I re-inflate them and what if the rims shred the tyres,what then?"

"You will have to go to a gawage and fill zem up again!"

"That's not happening mate, no, I'm not letting my tyres down. You'll have to take me back to Dover, back me off and put me on the top deck, just like I asked for when I booked on." It wasn't long before a small car arrived on the scene. It was the head of the Port of Calais, the main man.

"We will take the ship off this berth and put it on another berth to see if that will work." I could hardly believe my ears, the Chef Du Port de Calais coming out with the humdinger of the year.

"so what are you saying?"

 "We will move the ship to another berth and you can unload there, or maybe take you to Dunkerque if we must."

Dunkerque? was he really so dumb?

"And then what?" I asked.

"We will have to charge your company for the cost of moving the ship and all that entails."

"Charge me?" I was incredulous. "Charge me for what?"

"The ship, to move you to Berth 4 would be maybe £10,000 to Dunkerque or Boulogne, somewhat more....."

"You're not charging me a penny pal, your crew put me here, I told them beforehand to put me up top, but anyway, even if we sailed to Tangiers, it won't change the internal dimensions of the fucking ship, will it? I'd still be stuck because I'm stuck IN-side the fucking ship-not outside!"

I decided that I needed to walk away and leave them to fight amongst themselves, before I got arrested for punching someone stupid. It was another 20 minutes or more later that the penny dropped for them. I backed my truck up a little to where I had been during the crossing, then the ship filled with cars and trucks, everyone looking at me, because my truck was facing the wrong way. I was taken back to Dover and reversed off, only to reload again, on the same ferry, top deck, about 10 hours later. There was no charge, and I never saw the young lady who'd booked me on ever again. I got the load to Marseilles, intact, on time and without further ado, it's what I do you see, I get there, I do my job, it's what I'm paid to do.

Unlike some opportunists, I've never been one for helping myself from the load. If I'm offered wine, like we used to be, all the time in France, at one time, I would gladly accept it. All 'gifts' for the driver have always been welcome, it stops people from getting greedy or taking the most important part of the cargo. I don't see the benefit of taking £5 of something and then losing a £35,000 job, with little prospect of getting another, no, my pay was always what I banked on, whatever was in the back was under my charge, my responsibility to get it to where it was going, in one piece. Whether it was timber, steel, clothing, guitars, pharmaceuticals or whatever, it wasn't mine to touch, even the 26 pallets of new Euro banknotes I once picked up, everyone of them arrived safely in Denmark. Imagine that, 26 pallets of bank notes, I can't begin to imagine the actual value of that load. I do, however, know that one load I used to carry quite a lot was worth a large amount of money. We used to collect analgesia, *painkillers,* they were transported in blue plastic barrels, each one valued at £1,000,000. A full load consisted of 96 barrels, that's a lot of pain killers, and a lot (£96M) of responsibility.

As valuable as all these things seem, they are all replaceable, goods can be remade, rebuilt, replaced, people can't. The roads of the world are littered with the debris of a million deaths, millions of accidents and incidents occur daily, life for many, irreversibly changed or ended. I have been lucky, I'm still here to tell my tales, many aren't. The graveyards-as they say, are full of 'Heroes'.

2 Temple Of Love

Should I fall or should I cry, should I lie awake at night, should I see and not
believe in you, then step away now, step away.
If I grow cold and weary, my heart-turned black and still, if you see nought but fear for
me, step away now, step away.
When there's nothing left to see here, nothing left to feel, when there's only love in the
past tense, step away now, step away.

It was 40 degrees celcius when I left Eilat, barefoot, with just a rucksack of clothing, mostly Crew uniform consisting of T-shirts, sweatshirts and jogging bottoms. My yellow shorts with the cigarette hole in the back, heavily oiled and paint smeared, clung filthily around my skinny waist. I hadn't shaved in nearly 6 months, having long since broken through the itchy pain barrier of early facial hair. I was so very far removed from the young man who'd arrived in Israel barely a year before. I had lived a lifetime in a matter of months. Seen beauty in the desert, war in the Upper Galilee. I'd survived against the odds, no matter what had been thrown at me, I was still standing, although not necessarily the same person as when I came. It is simply not possible to be the same, to live through so much and be unchanged. Anyone who tells you to remember your roots, don't forget who you are, don't forget where you come from, has never been anywhere themselves. It's important to remember, but not to be shackled and restricted by one's past, the place of your birth is just that, a place, once in time. It's not a life long burden unless you make it so. In order to grow, develop, improve, mature and adapt, we must change, we must demand better than we had, better than we were, more than ever, life must develop in order for progress to be made.

I took a bus out of town, along the long desert road that ran parallel to the Egyptian border, through dusty mountains to the international airport known as Eilat Ovda. It was no more than a military airstrip in the middle of nowhere. A small tent city in the desert, a long way from the town I had left behind this one last time, along with my floating home - the Schooner, Zorba 1, refitted after a month in dry dock, complete with new keel, copper plated hull, a waterproof stern tube and new pulleys on her generator. Gone were the leaks, the burnt out impelors and broken bilge pumps, the Zorba 1 was as good as new, with her new 1st mate and skipper. I was headed back to

England, my Skipper, Mula, headed for the Seychelles. I had turned down his offer of going with him, tempting as it was, to work on a dive boat, with a proper wage. I had also turned down Dadi's offer to stay with Holiday Charters. Full Israeli citizenship in 1996 was a tempting offer, but I had a better one, I had a new start, another chance to make something of myself and my soon to be newborn Son. How could anything compete with that?

I landed on British soil, the cold air hit me immediately and my clothes proved to be far from ideal for the time of year. My dangly bits withered into little walnuts as the cold air tickled my throat. I was no longer in the Middle East, this was no warm welcome.

After a few days to readjust in a village on the outskirts of High Wycombe, Tara and I moved to Romford, I was back to square 1, back where it had all begun so many years earlier, the memories of my childhood clinging to every dark shadow and piss filled alleyway.

My first mistake was the desire to see my kids, that in itself was not the problem, I loved and missed them terribly always, especially when I was away. I had thought about and quietly cried for them every day since I'd left my marital home. Now I needed to see them, I was back in the country and had to get to Coventry, I had to see them, hold them, tell them I love them and then break their hearts once more. I had to tell them I wasn't coming back to live with them, that I would visit when I could, that they had a new little half-brother coming soon. That I would be leaving them again, once more, for the millionth time, I would hold them and then walk away.

We hugged, we cried, we talked and played something,a board game or some such diversion, the TV burbling in the background as always. Nikki cried, made drinks and disappeared upstairs. The girls were amused by my beard, they hadn't expected it, nor had they expected me to do anything other than come and go once more. I could tell by the distance between us all, we were no longer a family, probably, and in all honesty, never had been. I was too often absent, and now I had been gone a year only to return with a new pregnant partner. The scene was set for disaster, and a disaster it became. I so desperately wanted to stay, to try again even though I knew it was a bad idea. Nikki was just as highly strung as she had been before I left. She'd shaved her head at one point, an attempt to crop me from her life, stop the images and memories of me that occupied the inside of her head. Her hair had started to grow back, was short and naturally brown, a sort of mousey brown that nobody admits to having, except mice and hipsters. In 1997 there were no hipsters, just a generation of lost navel-gazing wasters, strung out on drugs that scared real drug takers. Everything was dirty, cheap and disintegrating.

When Nikki disappeared upstairs and I heard her crying, I should have left. I should have kissed the girls goodbye and let myself out. I should have done anything, anything other than try to stop her. I walked straight into her trap. How I could be so stupid I can't explain, honestly, I'm not a stupid guy,

I'm not so fucking daft as to fall for the oldest trick in the book, to feel sorry for her tears and to think that just for one moment it would ever be a good idea to lay with her, ever, for old time's sake, one for the road, one to remember before I go for the last time. I'm not that fucking stupid am I?

The answer came in a phone call just as I got home. I knew as the colour drained from Tara's face who it was that was calling, and I could see by the hate in her eyes that Nikki was telling her every sordid detail. How could I be so stupid? Why, when I had a whole new life in front of me, a new start, another chance to get it right, to settle down and raise a family of my own without making the mistakes my parents had, how could I…..?

The black eye eased within a few days. I deserved it, and more. Coventry was now off limits for me. I would probably never be trusted again and it was of my own doing. I had nobody to blame but myself, and a vengeful ex-wife. I can never condone what happened, I don't even understand it myself, or do I?

Maybe, after all is said and done, after all the niceties on the outside, inside am I just an animal after all? Do I take what is given, and if offered, accept. Is it that simple, or was there more to it, much more, like feeling I'd survived a trauma that had been tearing me apart for the last 8 years, and more than anything in the world needed a feeling of normality, of recognising something familiar, feeling 'At Home', wherever and whatever that was? Was this PTSD before it was given that name, or just an inability to keep it in my pants, was I really so lame? The truth is out there- they say, and I'm still looking for it. I know I was wrong, and that I would pay for it for the rest of my life, I know that. I won't excuse myself, I made a very bad choice and live with it to this day still, because some things are used against you, even when you know you were set up. Once the shock was over, I was told in no uncertain terms that this would be the only time I would ever be forgiven. It was also the only time I would ask.

 I needed to find a job, and quickly, there was no money and no chance of getting anything from the dole office, I had been out of the country and therefore didn't qualify for state assistance. I immediately made a few calls, some letters were sent out and interviews set up. I managed to get to see one company I knew but arrived a day late, only to find the truck (and therefore job) had left the day before for Kiev. Undeterred, I went to another company nearby, and filled out an application form. When I got home, there was a phone call from a couple who'd worked on one of the yachts in Eilat. They were in Holland but heading up to Sweden to pick up a boat they'd just bought, and could I join them? Could I?

"You know I'd love to, but what's the plan?" I asked.

"Can you get over to Sweden next week, we want to work on the boat, maybe 6 weeks or so, then we leave for Eilat."

I was about ready to dig my yellow shorts out of the bin, the ones with the cigarette burn in the bum, the very mention of the words 'Boat' and 'Eilat' had me almost peeing on the carpet, and I wasn't even the pregnant one in the house. This was what I wanted, so badly, not the soggy carpet, the phone call, the offer of another adventure.

"So how long are we looking at? I mean, it's quite a trek and all."

"I think we are looking at stopping off a few times on the way, we have no set time limit but maybe about 6 months to get there, maybe."

I was busting to say yes, but I couldn't. Tara was by now about 3 months pregnant, despite their offers to have her come too, she would struggle on such a long journey, in cramped conditions, pregnant, on a yacht at sea, having a baby between ports just didn't seem like a viable option.

"Thank you so much, but we just can't do it!" How I hated those words coming from my mouth. All I really wanted to say was -Yes.

Yes, of course, Yes. But the sensible little demon whispering in my sensible ear, said,

"No!"

Bastard....!

The next call was from John at Kentvale, the firm I'd popped into whilst passing on my way home.

"Hi, yes, I was wondering if you could go to Italy for me next week, ship out on Sunday?"

"Yes mate, of course." It wouldn't take 6 months to drive to Italy, I knew I'd be home in time for the baby's birth.

"Brilliant" I'll call you tomorrow to let you know more."

I had a job, I was back on the road having barely unpacked my backpack. I would have to rough it for a week or two until I had enough money for some new yellow shorts, without the cigarette burn in the bum, some things just never catch on with the masses, their loss not mine, I know I'm cool.

John rang again the next day.

"Been a change of plan, you're still shipping out on Sunday, but I'm sending you with another driver, you're both going to Budapest,Hungary, you've been before haven't you?"

"Yes, I've been there quite a few times, used to clear at Royal Sped, nice little job, that!" I'd been there regularly only a couple of years ago, but things change in transport, very quickly. "We used to go through Czech and Slovakia, it's cheaper than paying Austrian Taxes."

"We go through Austria, it's quicker and cheaper now we use Eco-Points."

Eco-Points were like Green Shield Stamps for truckers, instead of getting yet another cheap clothes, an Iron, or hair dryer that would burn out before your Alberto Balsam was blown dry, we'd use them to transit Austria without paying taxes, but they were only valid for transit runs, if delivering or loading in Austria, we didn't need them, as I was to find out on my third trip.

'Little' Stevie Coe, AKA Buddha, was a lovely guy, he was already in the yard Sunday morning when I arrived. He'd been a driver for as long as I had, and now that he was separated from his Mrs he decided to try European work for a change. He hadn't been with Kentvale for too long but knew his stuff, he was to show me-the new kid, how to do the job. We had a pretty uneventful trip, everything ran smoothly. Customs were quick and easy in Dover, followed by a smooth sailing to Calais. Nobody got stuck between decks, no roads were blocked, it was just as it should be. Our cargo consisted of 2 Land Rover Defenders each. Our transit was simple and uneventful, and on arrival in Budapest, Steve led us to a layby on the Eastern side of the city.

"We stop here for the night and our man will knock us up in the morning."

"What time is he coming?" I asked, wondering just how kosha this job was, after all, we hadn't cleared 'Into' Hungary yet.

"Don't worry, he'll knock us up when he gets here, just give him your papers and he'll be back an hour later to take us to the delivery site."

Sure enough, it all ran like clockwork, and our delivery was a little back street in a village about 10 minutes drive away. To unload the cars, we had to use a set of long heavy steel ramps that were stored inside the chassis of the trailers. It was back breaking work moving them around and I felt nervous about having set them up straight, if the car fell off as I drove down them, I would know I'd got it wrong. We were both empty and heading back into Austria in what seemed like record time. Our backloads were from LKW Walther, near Vienna, a short time later and we were finally homeward bound.

What used to be a 10 day trip via the Czech Republic, we had managed in 6 days, door to door. I was home Friday night and then back again to Hungary on Sunday. This time I took Tara with me, she'd never been in a truck and it was a novelty for her, it was good to get her out of the apartment too. Spending too much time alone, waiting is a claustrophobic affair, especially if you're in an unfamiliar place, as she was. Romford was a step down from High Wycombe, although both have their drawbacks and anyone can find trouble anywhere if they try enough.

We stopped for supper at the Mcdonalds on the newly extended MO, Budapest's only stretch of motorway stopped at the city when I had been going a few years before, now it turned south and ran down to the Romanian border, bypassing the 'Containers' truck stop that we all used to use on the National 5. We got a take out burger meal and returned to the truck. Within minutes there was a knock on the passenger door.

"Tell her to fuck off!" I said, I knew only one sort of person would be tapping on the wrong door of a British registered truck. Tara looked out at the girl and gestured for her to go away, which she did, but a few minutes later came back again. The second time she was shooed away only to return a third time. Tara wound down her window just as the young hooker opened her coat to show what was on offer.

"It's alright luv, I've got plenty of my own!" Said Tara, pulling up her Holiday Charters sweatshirt and proudly showing her own breasts. The prostitute ran back from whence she came and we were left to finish our milkshakes in peace.

My third trip saw me dropping myself in it. I'd called in when empty, outside Budapest, and was told there was no load in Vienna this time, I was to head towards Munich and I'd collect something around there. This meant I would need Eco-points to transit Austria, I hadn't been given any this trip and forgot all about them. At the border I was asked my destination.

"Munich" I said, innocently enough.

"You have Eco-punkts?"

"Eco-points? No mate, sorry I don't. I wasn't given any this time round-"

"You must have Eco-punkts for transit..."

"But I'm not transiting" I lied, thinking fast on my feet. "-I have to load in Vienna"

"You said Munich, Munich is in Deutschland, not Osterreich!" I really didn't need the Kindergarten level geography course, nor the disdainful look in the eye of this green uniformed servant of the state. I knew damn well where Munich and Vienna were, I also knew where the bloody points were as well, back home in John's office. I needed to talk fast and convince him it was a simple error.

"Look mate, when you asked where I was going, I thought you meant eventually, I didn't know you meant now, I'm going to Munich when I'm loaded, then I'll be stopping for the night, I just have to pick up some groupage first in Vienna." I surprised myself with this one, fuck me, I'm good.

"I want to see your load details, you cannot leave here until I have your load confirmation from the agent in Osterreich." Our conversation was over, he gave me a slip of paper with a fax number written on it. I was stuck on the border until I could prove I had a collection to do in Austria. I rang John.

"OK, leave it with me, I'll see if I can get LKW Walther to send something through, give me half an hour and then go back in...."

It was about 2 hours later that a fax arrived. The dubious border guard slowly read every word, double checked the details and looked at me knowingly. He knew as well as I did, that the paper he held was a forgery, there was no load in Vienna, someone had doctored a previous fax and changed dates and registration numbers, he knew, because I had told him the truth the first time round, I was going to Munich. Reluctantly, he allowed me to go.

The next week I was sent to Italy, then to Portugal, France and then followed that with a couple of trips to Germany. Time was moving on and Tara was getting bigger. The baby was due soon. I had taken the job with Kentvale to get back on the job market, but I was needed at home now. I was to be a father again soon, and that meant being around to help with things.

I got my brother Les a casual job with Kentvale before I left, it helped him out as he was a fireman and enjoyed some extra cash in hand work on his days off. It helped John too, gave him someone he could rely on at short notice to help in the yard or deliver/collect around the UK. Les got stuck in and I gave my notice, having found some agency work nearby. I left on good terms, meaning I would always be willing to do a bit for him if I was available, but I wasn't available full time as I was now needed at home.

I worked a couple of weeks on the Agency, night trunking to Warrington and back, then the phone rang again.

"Are you busy?" John asked.

"Not at the moment, why what d'you have in mind?"

"I have a driver in hospital in Spain, can you go and rescue his truck for me, reload is waiting near Bordeaux, just fetch it home for me if you would?"

"I reckon I could, when do you need me?"

"Get to the yard as soon as you can, I'll have you on a plane by lunchtime."

My instructions were simple enough, fly to Bilbao then get to Burgos any way I can, the Driver is in the Hospital with Liver problems, the keys are under the bonnet. John dropped me at Heathrow with an envelope stuffed with cash and no further instructions. Somewhere out there was a Kentvale truck, and I was going to have to find it.

There was no internet in those days, no Google Maps, just the hard knowledge learned from experience and the ability to work things out for ourselves. Adapt and survive.

I flew to Bilbao, found a travel map and decided on my route. I made my way to the train station and got a ticket to Burgos, via Madrid, there was no direct link so this was all that was available as an option to me. I changed trains in Madrid and headed back North to Burgos, where I hailed a taxi to take me the 15 or so kilometres out of town to the truckstop on the N1. I paid the driver and wandered around looking for a Kentvale truck. There were hundreds here, and with it now being late at night, I was quite aware of just how dodgy I was starting to look. I eventually found the truck and lifted the bonnet, there were no keys.

"Bollocks!" I cursed.

"What are you doing?" Someone was climbing out of the truck.

"Sorry mate, John sent me over to pick up his truck, the keys are meant to be here, under the bonnet."

"They were, but when John said you were coming, I discharged myself from the Hospital to get a lift home-knowing John, he'd leave me here if he could," Pete said. " And this is my Daughter-in-Law, Karen." Karen had stepped out from the shadows, expecting some level of trouble-no doubt, but I wasn't the thief in the night they had envisaged. I said hello and my mind did a fleeting calculation, suddenly there were 3 fully grown adults, even though Karen was as skinny as a rake, the sort of woman who stands with her legs together and can still get a bike between her thighs, there was no meat on her at all, her face was gaunt and pale. 'Maybe it was her that had been ill?' I thought. Pete read my mind.

"It's ok, we can sleep in the trailer on the way back, seeing as it's a bit cramped
 for space here."
We climbed into the cab, Karen hid behind the driver's seat, Pete sat uncomfortably on the passenger side, he was clearly not well, his face contorting occasionally as pains racked through his insides. I knew what he was going through and empathised with him as I settled into my position at the wheel. I filled out my tachograph card and fired up the Scanias engine.
"Mind if I smoke?" Pete asked, pulling out some tobacco.
"No, help yourself mate, I've quit but it doesn't bother me."
"No, do you mind if I SMOKE?" He emphasised the word so much I was expecting him to disappear behind a cloud, like Fenella Fielding in Carry On Screaming. I knew he was ill but I didn't know he had Vampyrism. He wasn't as nice to look at either, his red figure hugging dress had obviously been left at home, but as I shot him a glance across the cab, I saw the bag of green leafy substance he'd pulled from his pocket.
"Help yourself mate, just make sure there's none left when we ship back into England, and if there's any problems, I know nothing about it-Okay?"
"No I know, I won't have any left, I never do, I have to use this to control the pain you see-it's the only thing that helps. I'd never fetch any back with me though, just in case I get stopped by customs."
 It was one thing to be having to rescue someone who was poorly, but then to arrive and not only did he have his Son's wife with him, which was just a little bit odd, but that he was pothead too, it was kind of taking the piss a little bit, I felt as though Pete was actually meant to have been left behind, that John may actually have been done with him for some reason, that Pete had been tipped off and high-tailed it to the truck before the truck left without him.
 I set off into the dark, it was somewhere around the 2AM mark, not a busy time for trucks on the road in Spain. This meant a nice easy run up to Bordeaux in time to reload later that day, and if Pete is straight, or at least not dead, I could always put a disc in with his name on it to get us up to the ferry, if we were shipping back from Normandy. I was mid way through working the timings out when I was suddenly pulled back to my conscious self. Standing in the road, a few hundred metres in front of me was a policeman, a Red Cap as we called them, on account of their bright red berets, the blue lights of his van silhouetted his outline against the dark Spanish night.
"Fuuuuckk!" I hit the brakes and pulled up alongside him, hoping Peter would remember I knew nothing about the stash he had in his pocket. Thankfully I'd had the window open as I was driving so as not to get myself stoned or fall asleep as I was driving.
"Karen, stay still, don't say a fucking word, Peter, remember you're sick….." I leaned out of my window to talk to the guy who was undoubtedly about to send me straight to Spanish gaol, no passing Go, no collecting anything but a

few bruises, some olives and lots of new friends called José. I could already see myself shackled in the back of the van. I remembered quickly, the time when my old boss Malcolm had returned from a trip to Barcelona, sporting a nice new black eye and grin, "Took six of the fuckers down with me though..." He said, smiling. Was this to be my moment, scrapping with the Red Caps over someone else's pot?

"Disque Chofer, disque!" He wanted my tacho's. I pressed the eject button and out came my almost pristine card.

"Que?" He looked at the disc and compared it to my previous disc from England a couple of days previously. He looked at me quizzically as I handed him my boarding card. "Que?"

"I flew here, Avion, y'know, big plane, colleaga here, in Hospital, Burgos, malade, colleaga malade, me avion, Bilbao y trein a Burgos, now lading in Bordeaux...."

"Que?" I have no idea what language that was, or which he spoke, but I'd just tried communicating in about 5 different tongues with no recognition. "Donde esta los documentes?" He wanted my truck papers, I had to get them out to him quickly, without him stepping up into the truck, if I open the door now he'll take one sniff and I'll be reliving Midnight Express.

"Here," I passed him my folder, the one with all of Peter's delivery notes etc. He started to understand now what had happened, How it was I came to be here without having driven down.

"Okay, Okay, go!" He handed back the folder and I smiled.

"Muchas graçias, senór."

I drove for the rest of the night with the window open, I didn't care how cold it was on the bunk behind me, Karen would just have to wrap herself up in Peter's sleeping bag. Peter fell asleep and I sailed through the border at Irun, stopping only for coffee at a service area in the forest, a large area between Bordeaux and the Spanish border. It was notorious for speed checks, customs, and just about every Frenchman in a uniform of one description or other. I headed to our collection point and left the others to sleep while I loaded up. There seemed to be a lot of movement in the cab, Peter and Karen were obviously struggling to get comfortable laying so closely together on the single bottom bunk. Meanwhile, I was in the trailer loading 26 pallets of wine, this was a rarity for me, years before when I'd worked for Hoship, it was normal for us to do anything from 6 to 16 collections to make up a full load of wine, a full shoot was practically unheard of. Once loaded, I called John to get my shipping instructions.

"Run up to Calais mate, bring it to the yard and I'll have someone deliver it on Monday."

We stopped the night in a service area. Over dinner Peter told me about his Son, Karen's Husband. Peter had a strained relationship with him, he was a bit of a lad and would often knock Karen around. He was currently on a sabbatical, 18 months for Burglary and GBH, hence why Karen was with him, to get away and have a break from it all.

"We'll get in the trailer and sleep there, that'll be better all round for everyone" Said Pete, who was by now so healthy on the outside, I had to wonder what had actually sent him to the hospital in the first place, maybe he'd just had food poisoning, too much liquor, I didn't know, I just thought his recovery was pretty quick once I arrived on the scene.

It must have been a pretty windy night outside, the cab kept rocking and waking me from my slumber, the trailer seemed to be suffering the most, almost rocking in time to some music I wasn't able to hear, and it obviously had kept Peter and Karen awake, as they appeared for breakfast looking somewhat worn out.

Back home again, I had an interview with another agency, Online Roadways, only this time, I was offered a full time position working internally at Ford's factory in Dagenham, night shift, shunting trailers around the site, to and from the various buildings to the Trailer yard or the company's own dock. They had their own ferries come in twice a day, from Zeebrugge.

I liked the sound of this, local work, good money, regular hours and no long periods away from home, when the baby arrived, I would be on hand. It was just what I needed. Regular and routine, the two things I'd never had in my life before, I had always worked long hours with long periods away from home, never able to know for sure, where I would be or when, unless it related to my delivery schedule, homelife was something that was always on hold, until now. I had a routine, a regular 12 hour night shift.

Being the new guy on site I thought I may find it hard to mix with some of the other drivers, but that wasn't the case. I was warmly welcomed and helped to find my way around the site. I knuckled down and did my job, as required. By the end of the first week I felt pretty confident in my post, I was also promoted.

"The night shift supervisor is leaving, I want you to take over the job" said my new boss Steve, not in the least bit unsure I was the right man for the job.

"I've barely been here 5 minutes, the other's won't be too happy about that, will they-is there not anyone here already you wouldn't prefer? Someone who knows their way around and all the different jobs."

"No, they're a bunch of lazy bastards and cunts too when they want to be, No I want you to do the job so we have some fresh blood in there, and anyway, I trust you, you're a good worker, your foreman has kept me up to date with what's going on, who does what, who doesn't, that sort of thing, he speaks very highly of you!"

I was shocked, not by the colourful language, but because I'd made such an impression so quickly. I was to get a £10 per week rise, and my first ever mobile phone.

Back in 1996, mobile phones were not the sleak, slim, lightweight things of today. They were the size of a Mortar bomb, weighed the same as a polaris submarine and would have to be switched off during thunderstorms for fear of attracting a lightning strike. Nevertheless, possessing such a cool piece of modern technology, meant people looked up to you. We had only just come to terms with the fact that telephones would work without us being connected to the exchange by 15 miles of cable. This was nothing short of a miracle- a phone you could carry in your pocket. The price paid in return, was having to put up with carrying a house brick around in your opposite pocket, to balance out your jacket. The ring tone had no volume button, it would wake the dead within 600 metres, but to talk and be heard, you would often have to shout into the mouthpiece. Somedays, the invisible string between caller and recipient, would work perfectly, other times, 6 inches one way or the other could cost you to lose connection. Technology has come a long way in these last few years, if I wanted to share photos, I'd have to walk around clutching a photo album, which was basically a folder the size of a Stanley Gibbons Stamp collector's album, if you're on the youthful side of 45,ask your grandparents about that one….

Within the space of a few short months, I'd left Israel, had offer after offer thrown at me and somehow managed to find myself at the bottom of the food chain in my own ratings chart. A night shift supervisor, for a subcontractor, in the very factory I had spent all my life running away from. I had willingly become the fodder of my nightmares, the clock watching, walking dead prisoner of an industrial workhouse. How did this happen? I was a free man, I was a rebel without a brain- how could I have sleep walked into

this trap? The universe was conspiring against me, it was obvious, but there was a reason- there's always a reason, not that it's easily seen at the time, but there was a bloody good reason for me to be back in England, The Sex Pistols had reformed and were playing live. It had been 18 years or more since their infamous split after their final performance in San Francisco. The band I loved most, the band whose music had inspired me to get off my arse and bounce around, get up and live, chase those dreams and refuse to conform. They were back, and I was not going to miss them.

The first reunion gig had been in Finsbury Park, I'd missed that performance by being in Hungary at the time, working, but I was not to have to wait too long. Nikki had been at Finsbury Park and later told me how brilliant it was. So good, in fact, she got on somebody's shoulders and removed her top, flashing her gnat bites at Steve Jones, I doubt he would've noticed though.

I had to wait just a little longer to see them play at the Phoenix Festival, near Stratford-on-Avon, on a perfect summer's evening.

I had spent my whole life hoping to one day see them play, and they did not disappoint. The Sex Pistols were a musical force to be reckoned with. A powerhouse of beautiful noise that drives and pushes you ever onward. Their stance is one of pure adrenalin and bile, the warning signs are there- don't fuck with us, "We mean it Maaaan!" No bullshit, no pretence, you get exactly what you pay for, a breathtaking wall of percussion, a bass guitar that subliminally pounds through you like the blastwave of Tomahawk missile, the Sex Pistols were not for the faint hearted, they were loud, powerful and beyond anything I could have hoped to have achieved at their age. John Lydon, AKA Johnny Rotten, was a teenager when he wrote Anarchy In The UK. Seriously, that is some really clever song writing for someone of that age. Most teens-myself included, would barely have even heard of the word Anarchy if it hadn't been for the Sex Pistols, or News At Ten bastardising it's very meaning, it's got nothing to do with rioting, throwing bricks or petrol bombs, it's about mutual respect and doing as you please without impinging on another person's freedoms, but you already know that, you read it in My Book-Innit? Didn't you? I know you did.

Tara was very pregnant by this time, she came along to the festival, but didn't get too close to the stage, nor did she climb aloft anyone's shoulders and rip her top off. She stayed at a safe distance, along with Paul, an old ship mate from the Zorba 1, and ex-Dafna volunteer. He'd come along to see what all the fuss was about, having read my copy of Lydon's book, *No Blacks, No Dogs, No Irish.* It had been a christmas present the year before when we were in Eilat, almost a lifetime ago. I don't think he enjoyed it anywhere near as much as I did, it wasn't really Tara's thing either, but they both got a kick out of seeing me bouncing around and getting sweaty.

We spent the next few months pretty much locked up in a little apartment in Romford. Tara got bigger, the flat got smaller, I spent my spare time learning how to read navigation charts, studying for various qualifications in a bid to work my way up to becoming a professional yacht skipper. I passed the First Aid At Sea Certificate, RYA (Royal Yachting Association) VHF Radio Operator's Licence, Basic Sea Survival, Competent Crew and then the Coastal Skipper Certificate, I was determined to get back to the sea, return to Eilat as a family, with qualifications to earn a real wage doing what I loved best. I studied and worked hard, then when that was done, I was working 60 hours a week to pay for everything.

I have never been happy living around Romford, I put up with it, make of it what I can, but invariably I end up leaving again. There's a part of me so detached from the people and place itself. I am different, I know I am. I just do not fit in with the people there. One evening, we'd been shopping and were waiting outside the store. The place had to close up due to a power cut that knocked out most of Dagenham too. Standing by the bus stop an old lady next to us turned to her friend and said:

"Look Beryl, it can't be too bad- the lights on the bus are working!"
I just.......

Can't.......

3 Born Too Loose

Jordan

And in my dreams when sleeping
When walls have gone to ground,
In times of tears and feeling,
Hopelessness, the friend I've found.
I see your eyes and I see
The years I left behind,
The fears that haunt my daydreams
Long lost in this state of mind.
Will you stand beside me
Will you walk this way?
Will you never know these
Tears I cry for you each day?
Don't look beyond the darkness
The clouds I hide behind,
The rain that keeps on falling
Soft and sweet these tears I cry.
And still you stand there waiting
Your shadows blend with mine,
Our voices linger slowly
Splintered lives moved on in time.

"Push and breathe….."

"I am pushing you fucking idiot, you wanna try this? Do you?"

Tara's nails were drawing blood on the back of my hand, her grip tight enough to meld solid steel plate and timber, this was not the delivery we were expecting. The birthing pool was fully booked, it was too late for an epidural and god knows I needed it. There was only oxygen at this point, and Tara was hogging that to herself, where the fuck was my pain relief?

"I swear to god, you're never putting that thing near me again.. Aaaaghhh!"

"Is it time yet nurse?" I asked the Midwife.

"Not yet, she's nearly there, keep breathing, my lovely, keep breathing"

"I keep telling her that and she keeps swearing at me."

The Midwife looked at me sideways.

"What did you expect, you're a man? You did this, now look after her!"

Me? My fault? I didn't do anything except…..

"Fuuuuuuuuuuuuuu…...Aaaaaaghhh!"

Tara sucked hungrily on the oxygen mask, a red line scored over her face as her body tensed with the next contraction. I looked over to her Mum, sitting politely beside the bed, my eyes pleading for help. Surely this wasn't right, I didn't remember Sian and Christina's births being quite this painful, or drawn out, it had been a few hours since we came in to the hospital, Tara having gone beyond her term and now, having been induced, the birth was more complicated than we'd hoped for. Surely Pat could see it, she's a woman, a mum, she knows about these things, doesn't she?

I looked back at Tara, her face flushed and sweat had started to bead on her skin. My mouth opened but nothing came out.

"Here," said Pat, taking her daughter's hand. "You've got this, come on, breathe with me, come on, with me!"

Pat was suddenly in charge, she hadn't just stepped up to the mark, she took complete control of the situation. The small, meek, blond haired mother who was often more scared of her own shadow, suddenly became a force to be reckoned with. She was in control, totally, and I was gobsmacked, I'd never seen her so assertive, ever. Tara responded well to her mother's intervention, she still gripped my hand tightly enough to make me think my bones had been splintered, I was certain I'd never be able to bend my fingers again, that I was permanently disfigured from the wrist down. Wanking was definitely no longer on the cards.

"Ok my lovely?" The midwife had eventually returned and taken us seriously at last, there were other women giving birth, but we were all expected to wait our turn and perform when it was mutually convenient for the hospital staff. "Let's get you down to the delivery room".

No matter how much you plan for a birth, no matter how much you insist on having this or that course of pain relief or style of birth, it never happens that way, babies have an uncanny way of coming out when and how they will. In the case of Jordan, he decided he was quite happy where he was, warm, cosy and safe, he was so happy where he was, that he rolled around when the time came for his birth, wrapped his umbilical cord around his neck and bungied up and down Tara's birth canal. Eventually it was decided that intervention was needed and out came the blades. Jordan was born by Caesarean section and was whisked away immediately, I just caught a glimpse of him, blue and almost lifeless. The theatre team were well practiced experts at blocking and diverting my attention. Our Son was removed and things done of which we had no idea, even after being returned a few minutes later.

"What's wrong, where's my baby?" Tara begged.

"I don't know, I don't know what's going on." I couldn't see what was happening, I was still in Tara's vice-like grip and my view was obstructed by people in blue gowns doing things around our son, right in my line of vision. I sensed the relief in the room when he finally cried, and without delay, he was returned to Mum, still a little off colour. The cord that had given him the gift of life had almost cost his life, even before it had begun.

My first call, once mother and baby were settled, was to my own Mum. Pat and I then went to see her at her 'boyfriends' house. I'd never met him before, and Pat had never met my Mum. I knew they were chalk and cheese, but now they were both Grandparents to the cutest little baby ever born in the history of the world, I thought they'd use this common ground to bond.

"Now don't you let this one stop you from seeing your kids, not like that other cow did, you've got to get yourself a backbone and be a man,stop being such a pushover!" Mum had a way with words and diplomacy. Pat sat graciously, quiet and calm, unfazed. Her feathers may have been ruffled but she wasn't letting on. Pat could play the long game.

"We're going to call him Jordan."

"That's nice, what time's visiting hours in the morning? I want to come after work, about lunchtime."

"Just come when you're ready, they're pretty easy with visiting times." Mum worked in a care home, looking after elderly people, not the nicest of jobs but it kept her going and paid the bills. She held out a letter that had been sitting on the dining table, strategically placed and politely ignored.

"As if there's not enough going on, now I've got to go for another test, they're saying all of us are at risk of this thing, can't even go to work these days without catching something, I don't know what I'd do if I lose my job."

I looked briefly at the letter but couldn't take it in, it was from the Health trust she worked for, blah, blah, blah, caution, blah, something else, blah, MRSA, blah, blah, yours sincerely, blah! I passed it back, Pat and I were none the wiser, and anyway, we were still trying to get over the bungee birth of my Son, mum's problems were her own. We stayed a short while, and politely left. As soon as we got into the car I turned to Pat.

"I am so sorry for that, I don't know why she had to say that in front of you, I know Tara wouldn't do anything like that."

"It's okay, I was a little annoyed but- I mean she doesn't even know me and yet, well, don't worry about it, let's just get back and settle down for the night."

Next morning I called the hospital to see how 'Mother and Baby' were coming along. Both were fine albeit a little tired, sleeping in a postnatal ward is more of an ambition than possibility. As one infant settles, another demands feeding, burping or changing, the noise and smells are continual and the lights never go out.

"Mum sends her love, she seemed pretty excited," I exaggerated, "she's popping in straight from work to see you both."

"That'll be nice, I'm shattered but I should be alright later."

"Oh, she said something about having to get checked out for something, I don't know, something about work. Have you ever heard of MRSA? It might be worth asking the nurse about it, I ain't got a clue."

It was true, I'd never heard of Meticillin-Resistant Staphylococcus Aureus, in fact, not many people had, except for about 70% of the population who had either read the newspapers that particular week, or had been watching the TV News, neither of which were on my priority list as my partner was going into labour. I had barely settled back on the sofa when the phone rang again.

"Hello?"

"Can you tell the nurse here what you just told me?"

"Huh?"

"Tell what you said, about your mum."

"Oh that!" I replied, grateful it wasn't "I love you too honey bunny, I wish I could…." As much as I like nurses, it would be better to get to know one a little before telling them some things.

"I am sorry, but if your mother is at risk of having, or carrying MRSA, she cannot come onto this ward, and would not be welcome anywhere on the hospital grounds!" The Nurse was quite adamant, this was a big deal.

"Oh I don't think she's got it, she just has to….."

"If she works with people who may be at risk, she cannot come here, the fact that she has a letter rules her out of attending the hospital, this is a serious infection Mr Reid, it could kill people on this ward."

She wasn't messing about, this was bad news.

"Bollocks, I shouldn't have said anything!" I thought to myself, "how am I going to tell her she can't come?"

There was no Google, no way of referencing MRSA, short of asking a professional or going to the library, I'd done the first and the second would have been a waste of time as it probably hadn't been a known problem, until now. I had to go with what I'd been told.

"So anyway, Mum, she said you mustn't come to the hospital, it's not safe".

"What d'you mean not safe? I ain't got nuffink wrong with me, I'm coming to see my Grandson, she ain't gonna stop me from seeing my little boy…" The phone went dead and I knew the shit was about to hit the fan. By the time Pat and I made it to the hospital it was already too late. Mum had arrived unannounced and walked into the ward. Tara screamed for help and the other new mum's all began screaming. All hell broke loose. Tara was crawling up the wall in reverse, clutching baby Jordan to her breast. The other mums had each

grabbed their babies and were trying to get as far away from the crazy Grandmother with the infectious bugs, as they could. A nurse arrived, and another, everyone was yelling at everyone else and nobody was listening.

"I want to see my grandson….."

"You can't be here, you could kill us….."

"You have to leave here now!"

"You can't stop me from seeing my Grandson!"

"Get her away from me!"

Shrieks and screams tore through the ward, babies woke and cried as if to join in and say "Hey, I'm here, I have a voice too".

"No one's stopping me from seeing my Grandson!"

The crazy lady was eventually ejected from the ward and escorted from the hospital, the ward cleansed with bleach, Mum's and babies washed, everything covered in disinfectant, not that this would have defeated the MRSA bugs, but to give a sense of well being to those involved and at most risk of contracting infections. MRSA was also known as the Flesh Eating Bug, once it gets into an open wound, it would feed on the very processes that would normally heal that wound, the C-section ward of a maternity unit would be the perfect place for it to cause most harm. For reasons only known to herself, my mother had put every one of those women at risk that day, as well as my partner and newborn Son, something I could not excuse. It was to be many years before that bridge could be rebuilt.

Tara and I moved out, Pat gave us a room at her house on the outskirts of High Wycombe. It was time to start afresh, again, back to square one. I was in new territory. London was out of bounds, I couldn't live in the city again now, too many temptations for me. Coventry was off limits too, I could never go near the place while Nikki was still there. I was persona non grata with my own family, there was nowhere to go, I was alone but for my Son, his mother and her family, my former life was gone, everything removed or placed off-limits.

First things first, as always, I needed to get a job. It would have to be something nearby as I had no car. My hopes for finding work were very slim, I didn't have any knowledge of the area, had no car, no contacts and no income to make any of the necessary changes.

Tara had an older sister, Nicky, *No not that one….* This Nicky came with an added bonus, her boyfriend was a mechanic and had access to cars for sale, all I had to do was ask him to get me something cheap and reliable, the problem there was catching Adey when he was sober, not an easy thing to do. Adey liked his beer, he did a lot of business in the pub and according to Nicky, *(No, not that one….)* he didn't do very much business at home.

Thankfully though, I didn't have to wait long. Tara's Aunt was upgrading and sold us her old car, I was back in business, I had wheels and that meant I could get a job, once I got my car insurance sorted. I hadn't had a car for a few years and my license was heavily laden with 10 penalty points. I was one speeding ticket away from losing my license thanks to an accident I had in London a few years earlier. I'd come back from France and having spent the weekend in Dover, delivered my load of wine all around the south, finishing with a delivery in South London. Once empty I was told to head home. I knew London fairly well, or so I thought. Desperate not to get stuck in heavy traffic, I thought I'd sneak through the back streets of the West End, bad mistake. There are no shortcuts in the West End, not when you're pulling a 13.6 metre long trailer. So there I was, trying to turn left out of a narrow street with parked cars all around, as the trailer swung out the rear under-run bar dug into a parked car. Bollocks.

"There goes my fucking bonus!" I thought. I pulled forward and trashed the back end of the car. People were already all over me for holding up the traffic, but none had wanted to tell me as my back end was going to connect with the car, they just stood and watched. In my irritated state, I wrote a note on a scrap of paper and put it in an envelope.

"Are you going to move this thing Pal?"

Someone was behind me, then another voice.

"You hit that car!"

I scrambled around in the cab looking for my insurance papers and gave up in frustration. I shoved the envelope in my pocket and returned to the damaged car.

"Just leave your details mate, then get that thing out of here."

I put my hand in my pocket and pulled out an envelope, placed it on the windscreen behind the wiper, then left somewhat red-faced. I called the office and passed on the good news. I said I would have to go to the Police Station and report what had happened.

"No need, come here in the morning and we'll do it through the insurance, you've got the details haven't you?" The boss seemed remarkably calm, maybe he'd had a good day, unlike myself. I arrived home and emptied my pockets before having a bath, pulling out an envelope with a note inside:

'Sorry about your car, telephone number….." If I had the note, what had I put on the car?

Next morning the boss took a statement from me and filled out an insurance claim. It was to be another 3 months before I heard about it again, by which time, I quit that job. My boss hadn't passed on the insurance claim form, the police had tracked me because the guy who'd been in such a hurry to get me going, who'd distracted me into picking up the wrong envelope, was a police officer who'd noted my registration plate. 10 points for failing to report an accident. Failing to pull the right envelope from my pocket.

When I sent off my license to change my address, for the umpteenth time, I was delighted to find it came back clean, the points were gone. I had a clean ticket, a car and a job interview in Slough.

For reasons best known to themselves- they were desperate and I was available, I was offered a job immediately, given a uniform and a rota, 4 days on 4 days off, days, evenings and nights. I was back in the game, a fully fledged card carrying member of society, all I needed now was to stop thinking, switch off my brain, unplug my artistic streak and die quietly without anyone noticing.

My new job was to trunk 26 pallets of confectionery directly from the factory to a warehouse in Bicester. At both ends of the journey I had to back up dead straight onto a special bay. The trailers were fitted with chain floors, not a Saturday night special, kinky bondage type thing, but a set of chains that ran the length of the trailer, carrying the load onto and out of the trailer mechanically. Once lined up correctly, a special lead was plugged into the back of the trailer to power the motor, and in just under 90 seconds the load was gone, unloaded into a fully automated warehouse. Every pallet had a predetermined place, every load timed in and out to perfection, everything accounted for and stored in a computer somewhere in the building. Most of the time everything went like clockwork, no problems at all, but a wonky trailer could tip the load off the chain floor in the warehouse. The trailers had to be dead straight.

There were other benefits to the job too, freebies. Boxes and boxes of free chocolate. We didn't steal them, they'd be given to us by the warehouse staff, boxes that had been damaged in production, fallen off the line or simply 'sampled' somewhere in the factory. We could also buy chocolate in the work's shop, bags full of Mars bars, Bounty, M&M's, Snickers, Topic and other goodies, all at ridiculously low prices. Our wardrobe soon creaked under the weight of all those billions of calories, the bedroom smelled of Galaxy milk chocolate and it wasn't long before I could eat no more of it. Too much of a good thing is a reality, it becomes less and less attractive.

"'Ere, did you see them Tarts earlier?" Dilbert asked, "Phwoooaarrr! I would"

Somehow though, I doubted they'd reciprocate. Dilbert was a line operator in the factory, he'd sit in the driver's waiting room for as long as he could before waddling back into the factory. Dilbert was a year or two younger than myself. He still lived at home, belched loudly without warning and was the first person I'd ever come to know who couldn't reach his own wedding tackle. He weighed in at about 25 Stone, some 350lbs or 160kgs depending on whether you used bags of sugar or potatoes to work out what a bag of potatoes or sugar weighs. Dilbert had a stomach that hung almost to his knees, yet still managed to believe he was a worthy catch for any "Tart".

"That geezer with the flashy BMW, he runs a porno channel from over there." Dilbert pointed towards the row of small trading units opposite the loading bays. It was a badly kept secret that some of the units were allegedly studios used to broadcast the Babestation TV channel. I'd never heard of Babestation, and looking at some of the models going in and out of the building, I doubted any of them were Mothers, none of them carried changing bags or even turned up for work with their Babes in tow.

There were times at work, when I really felt out of place with those around me. Only one other driver, Ed Savage, had done any international work. Ed had been a Wagon and Drag driver for David Croome. He would often go to places beyond the Ural Mountains, places few Westerners would ever venture. To Ed, six weeks on the road was a normal shift, an 8 hour shift running to Bicester 2 or 3 times a day was the blink of an eye. He did it for the money, not for any sense of duty or love for the job, there was no love, only clock watching until it was time to go home. His adventures had all been 'Out there' in lands that none of his coworkers would ever see. I was the closest thing to normal for him, and we got on well whenever we shared a coffee in the small waiting room we seemed to spend so much time in.

Since returning from Israel, I'd spent a lot of time studying for my Royal Yachting Association (RYA) certificates. I'd managed to learn- or relearn, all the things I'd forgotten since leaving the Sea Cadets as a teenager. I had this desire to get back to the sea, to go sailing again. I'd also started a new course, Creative Writing. Like most things in life, I fell into this by accident. Having stopped on a motorway service area one day for a lunch break, I decided for some strange reason to buy a Trucking magazine, aptly named Trucking International. The last time I'd seen one was when I was working for Kentvale and it seriously pissed me off, not for any reason you'd imagine, but because it contained an article about a group of drivers who'd driven to New York, from Firenza, Italy, without getting a ferry. Six Unimog vehicles left Italy and headed North to Moscow. From Moscow they headed East and kept going into the bitter Siberian winter. They drove right to the end of the world, The Bering Straits, and they kept going. Although illegal, it was still possible to drive across the ice covering the Bering Sea, from the most Easterly point of Russia, to the most Westerly point of America, Alaska. From there it was a simple jolly South then East, all the way to the Big Apple. I was pissed off, I wanted to do it, I wanted to be that trailblazer, the guy who could drive to anywhere in the world, just give me a reason and I'll go.

I bought myself a magazine and flicked through, a story caught my attention and I began to read about a driver whose life would never be the same again-his bacon sandwich was cold, or he was panicking about getting to a layby in time to have a 45 minute break. It was such a petty irrelevance that I felt incensed and wanted to write to the editor. If that was all that was needed to spoil that driver's day, how the hell would he have ever survived my trip to Istanbul a few years earlier? I allowed this thought to whizz around my head for the rest of the day, *"pathetic, that was all it took for you to write about it and tell the world how hard done by you are? Really? Fucking UK truck drivers are a bunch of fucking wimps-look at you, yes you in that shiny Scania with your light bars and your chrome testicles, yes, YOU!"*........

I sat down at home and began to write. The whole of that awful journey revisited through my eyes. It was there, on 6 pages of lined A4 paper. The excitement, the dramas, trials and tribulations, I'd written every word from the heart, it was my story, my survival, my trauma, something I'd not really accepted before, that it was or had been traumatic. I'd lived in denial of that fact for a couple of years now, pretending all was ok, but deep down inside I was the kid from The Wall, the Pink Floyd film, left alone *"out there in the cold, getting lonely, getting old, can you help me?...."* Out there, beyond the white cliffs, way out beyond the safety of German precision and control. Beyond the castles of Bohemia and Moravia, past the plains of the Hun, somewhere beyond the Danube, a little lost boy had cried and nobody heard him.

I folded the sheets neatly, put them in an envelope and posted it the next day. The little boy had finally placed his message in a bottle, it was now the time of the tide to do its job. It was to be another few months before I stopped to treat myself to another magazine. Trucks were something I spent enough time around, I didn't really fancy myself reading about them as well. I had always written poetry and songs, usually pretty badly, for some reason I felt like a Bowie or Lou Reed for another generation, full of artistic prose and description, but in reality it was more like the amateur ramblings of a dyslexic dustman. Shelley and Dumas were never in fear of being usurped by my pen. However bad my scribblings were, to me they were my babies, the very essence of my being. Once I was dead, my words would live on and the kids would line the streets and cry on each anniversary of my falling.…..

The Ego is a wonderful thing, it protects you from the harsh reality of existence, makes you believe your own bullshit and creates an alter ego that consumes the old self allowing it to become the Hyde to your very own Dr Jekyll. My ego allowed me to think my words had meaning, relevance and were worthy of expressing, enough so that I signed up to a creative writing course. So that I could make a living from putting pen to paper, the reality was nothing like it. Of course I could write, of course my poems made sense to me, I'd read them a million times and become very exposed to the random meanings and twisted, poorly laid out script, I knew what I was on about if nobody else did, and if they didn't? Well tough shit to them for not having an open mind like I had, being able to understand the stories behind the veiled words. I would show them around, get people to tell me they were good and that I should get them published.

Living now in Buckinghamshire, I was surrounded by people who earned a living from the media. Wealthy actors, musicians and celebrities of all shapes and sizes are scattered throughout the Chiltern hills and down along the Thames Valley. It was just a shame I never knew any. Their presence was all around, reflected in house prices, rents and the cost of living generally. Everything seemed so much more expensive here than anywhere else I'd lived.

I used the invisible presence of the talent around me to inspire and urge myself ever onwards, I bought a copy of The Writer's And Artists Yearbook. I sent out letters to publishers, and collected a pile of rejection slips, nobody seemed interested in poetry anymore and eventually I stopped sending out the letters. I concentrated instead on writing songs, turning some poems into songs and writing new material. It was a pastime I loved and whenever inspired, I could just write a whole song in minutes.

Writing and studying to become a Yachtsman kept me going. They gave me hope, a lifeline to a better future. The present, it seemed, was so bloody dull that there had to be something more. It was the late 1990's and music was dead. Unless you were into warehouse raves, parties on farmland broken up by police raids, cocaine, ecstasy and the other mind-bending drugs now flooding the market, the scene that I'd loved all my life was dead on its feet. The new bands were products of the system, set up for money making, not for the love of music or for political and social change. Punk was dead, consumed and spat back out by the very establishment it was meant to tear down and replace. The fracturing of the movement, from Punks to Anarcho-punks, Goths and Vegans, the racist bootboys of the Oi movement who'd returned to the football terraces, their boots and braces were tired, worn out and beyond repair. It was not a time for standing out in the crowd, everything was underground, understated and totally misunderstood. The spandex invasion and longhairs of the 1980's had been sent packing, Killing Joke were lost in the wilderness, nobody wanted to put their heads above the parapet anymore, all our heroes were dead, dying or in rehab. There was a new TV show aimed at finding the next BIG Thing, Pop Idol. People were able to interact by calling a pay-to-use telephone number on their screens, thus financing the production of the show as well as the machinery to propel the winner to a guaranteed No.1 hit in the charts. It was an updated Opportunity Knocks, Ready Steady Go, and any number of other introductory talent shows. It was the death of independent music. It was shit. Manufactured garbage for the mindless masses, and there seemed to be no alternative to it, not in sleepy Buckinghamshire. Life, as I had lived it, on my terms, was over, slipping further away into my memory. There was nothing else for it, we had to get married.

Jordan was crawling around the floor, eating everything he could put in his mouth, getting bigger, faster, heavier and hungrier all the time, it was obvious Tara would have to make an honest man of me. The highlight of our week was eating out at the Indian restaurant, life was truly over and done with, I proposed and she accepted, I think, or had she made an executive decision? Either way, a date was set for the event of the century, a weekend nobody would ever forget, August 30 1997.

4 White Wedding

But I'm Down And I Hurt

I Shudder at your touch recoil from the fee

Of your fingers on my skin I know what you want

But I can't let you in.

Running from your love I hide from what's real

But I can't let you knowThat I know what you want and I can't let you in

'Cos I'm down and I hurt cried all I'll cry

Loved all I'll love now my heart,hearts bled dry

I've craved for your touch I've loved how you feel

Your tongue on my skin,I knew what you want

And I'd always give in.

So cold am I, so hard-it's true

To take what I give, to force it on you

My stag night consisted of an evening in the pub with Stuart, my soon to be (Step) dad-in-law. We swallowed a few beers and I eventually fell into bed. It was only in the morning that I realised how many beers a few can actually be. My head was banging and I swore 'Never again', that faithful old ditty spewed out so frequently by over-indulgent drinkers, 'Never again' until the next time, the next time being the very next day in this case. It was my wedding day, I had to partake of a tipple or two, or three.

The wedding itself was a small affair, the In-laws, a handful of friends and the registrars. We were given a cream coloured vintage Rolls Royce for the journey to and from the registry office, Tara had a cream coloured wedding dress and I wore the traditional suit and top hat as required by people with no idea how ridiculous I felt. I would have prefered a kilt and Dr Martens boots, but I doubt Tara would have made it down the aisle without tripping on the carpet, and the dress was too small for me anyway. We did the whole speeches and first dance nonsense, my two left feet Tangoed nimbly while my newly promoted wife Waltzed around the room to some ballad I can't even remember, I had thought about having 'White Wedding' by Billy Idol as our song but there was a distinct lack of virgins in the room and Highway To Hell would have been too premature at that point in our marriage. Drunk, overfed and totally out of place, the cream coloured Rolls Royce took us away to our Honeymoon suite at the local Holiday Inn.

Sleep came quickly and with it the innocent pleasure of not knowing what was happening in the outside world. Just a couple of hundred miles away, history was being made for all the wrong reasons, a story was breaking even as we fell so innocently into our pit. Just across the Channel, in a Paris tunnel, Princess Diana, estranged wife of Prince Charles, heir to the British throne, her new squeeze, Dodi Al-Fayed and their driver, Paul Henry, died following a high-speed chase through the streets. News of the incident had spread far and wide overnight, the whole world seemed to be silent, a morning in mourning. We awoke to a world without heart, a cold, unspoken anger seethed invisibly behind the stonewall of silent motion, even the M40 motorway outside the hotel window made little to no noise. It was as though Christmas morning had been delivered in the middle of a late summer. Silence clung in the air like a deep fog, heavy and uncertain, nobody, nothing wanting to break the spell. I had felt this silence before, when visiting Dachau Concentration Camp. The cold silent air of death was everywhere, in our hotel room, the corridor, the dining room, the entire outside world seemed cloaked in it. I sensed something was wrong and when I went to the reception area and saw the front page of all the newspapers I couldn't quite believe what I was seeing. Diana, dead? Diana was a true icon, she was of my generation, just a young woman finding her way through this world any way she could. A real-life Princess living the dream. The hierarchy had used her and spat her out, now she was dead, well and truly removed from the family business, never again to embarrass those whom she'd thought were family.

Tara and I were driven to Gatwick airport after a very stunted breakfast. Jordan remained at home with Pat and Stuart. There was little if any conversation in the hotel dining room, nobody had yet processed the news fully, nobody was ready to express their opinion or feelings on the matter, the world was not prepared for such a shock. Even the road seemed to pass silently by Uncle Jim's car windows. Jim was a nice guy, a sales rep for a printing company in Oxford. We hit it off immediately when we first met, especially when we found out one of his best mates owned the company who made the miniature railway I'd taken to Sicily a few years earlier, another example of the smallness of the world we live in. At the airport, Diana's picture was all over the front pages of all the newspapers. The cloud of uncomfortable silence hung over the departure lounge, it seemed nothing would ever be the same again.

Now don't get me wrong, I'm no flag waving Royalist, far from it. I see the Royal family as the descendants of the local bully-boys, the guys in the tribe too idle to do anything but steal and threaten everyone else until they gave them protection money/food/status. Royals are not descended from Gods, they're mere mortals who use others to do their dirty work, in this case, the Army, Police, Government and Secret Service Personnel. They are dangerous. They are the Status Quo, a continuation of oppression and force, woe betide anyone who may get in the way.

We landed in Orlando, Florida, collected our bags and rental car, then I drove us out to our motel, somewhere on the outskirts of Kissimmee. We'd chosen to be away from the town and parks, knowing there was a high risk of noise, burglary and general unpleasantness the closer to the parks the hotels were. Tourists were targets for all manner of stitch-up artists. One well known scam at this time was the slick selling of Timeshare Holidays. People would be lured into pseudo-evangelical style seminars, a sign offering 'Free Breakfast' and 'All you can eat buffet' would be enough to fill a church sized hall with hungry, expectant holiday makers-everyone of whom would have gladly sold their family car for just one more free Donut. Now you and I both know, nothing is really free, but there was a room full of people there the day we attended, hoping that breakfast was going to be just that-Free. But there was a huge price to pay. Once all the flair and bullshit was stripped back, the mathematics did their job revealing the true cost of the offer being pushed very vigorously around the room. Each Timeshare was actually cheaper than the full cost of a holiday to Florida, but only if taken 3 times a year, every year for 20 bloody years-can you imagine that? Groundhog day every fucking vacation you ever take. The same flight, the same 4 walls, the same parks, the same scenery, the same fucking flying bugs eating you alive 3 times a bloody year, it would be torture, and the price, don't even think about that, unless you could afford to bear a second mortgage to pay for the privilege of being bugfood 3 times a year.

"So where are you guys from?" asked the fat schmooze assigned to sign us up to 20 years of Groundhog Holidays.

"Buckinghamshire" said Tara, ignoring the fact that I was an unhappy Essex boy. Unhappy because, well, Essex…..

"I'm from England too, been here about 6 years now, I love it!" I could tell he loved the food, judging by the way his organs were stretching his 4XL shirt to the point the buttons could be classed as illegal ordnance, just one sneeze and he could've taken out half the room with a good ricochet.

"Whereabout in Essex?" I asked, he didn't look much older than myself and I thought we may have some common ground.

"Rainham, do you know it?"

"Yes, very well, I was brought up in Hornchurch." I wondered if he knew any of my old school mates.

"I know Hornchurch, yes, small world. I used to be a Limo driver, private hire, y'know parties and stuff, used to get some great rides and some of the stories I could tell you, Man, we could be here all day. But anyway, about our Holiday share plan…."

"Would it be okay if we had some more coffee, I just want to get another Donut first…" I walked over to the table with the donuts and pastries on, took a look around the room at the hard-selling going on at every other table and knew we were in for much of the same. It was going to be hard to get out of the room without signing anything.

"So as I was saying…."

"I don't think we'll be able to sign anything today" I cut him off, "I mean, it's a nice offer and all, but I think we'd like to have different holidays in different places."

"But if you sign up to this other plan, you can arrange to swap holiday destinations and times with other Shareholders, you just contact them and swap between yourselves as often as you like." I could see his buttonhole stretching further, he was ready to send out a burst of killer plastic, or fart, one or the other, neither of which I really wanted to experience.

"So what we'd be doing essentially, is buying 20 years of holidays in advance, is that right?"

"Yes, by signing the Direct Debit order, you're actually safeguarding yourself against future rises in the cost of your holidays, as well as any change in the exchange rate" He smiled.

"But rates go up and down, what if we lose out?"

"No, if the rate goes against you this year it might go for you next year, it all pans out over time, I've seen it go up and down in my time here, but nothing really changes, you get a guaranteed holiday, in a guaranteed holiday home at a guaranteed price year-in, year-out, you can't lose."

"But we may not want to come here 3 times a year...." I reminded him.

"Why not? It's great here, you love it, right?"

"Not so much I'd never want to holiday anywhere else, I don't think we'll be signing anything today, thanks for the breakfast and the coffee, but we're done here, we're going to get on with the rest of our holiday."

We got up and left the room just as an announcement came over the PA system that Judie and Eric from Wakefield had signed their contract.

September in Florida meant a very predictable weather pattern. The mornings were hot and humid, bug bites were very scratchy and sore until a suitable layer of cream had been worked into the skin. By midday the air was hot and dry, surprisingly comfortable and bug free, but at 3pm dark clouds rolled over and almost at the stroke of 4pm the heavens would open, torrential rain, thunder and lightning, skidding cars and fender benders, rivers flowing along the gutters and sidewalks. By 4.30pm the taps were turned off, the rain stopped and the sky cleared. By 5pm the bugs were out and it was time to get behind the fly nets. This was our daily weather routine, we could set our watches by it.

I'd never been to Disneyworld, I'd been to Disneyland Paris, prior to it's opening. having to deliver the Judge's podium for the Rodeo show a few years earlier, inadvertently chewing up the tarmac on the newly laid car park as I turned my truck around. I had never been a paying customer, it had never really appealed to me to be honest. Now that we were here, I thought it might be worth a visit just to say we'd been.

I followed the signs and drove for miles until we finally made it into a parking space in the car park. This place was huge, the car park itself was about the size of Coventry, with a bus service to take us to the gate. Once there we joined a queue 10 abreast, a mile long moving slowly forwards and eventually into the park itself.

"Look, there's the castle, and that's the zipwire Tinkerbell comes down at the end of the parade." Tara knew far too much about this place already, she'd done her homework and I remained ignorant to all about me. Her enthusiasm knew no bounds, she was in her own Nirvana. To me, all I could see were islands of different themed constructions in a river of people gleefully throwing money at everything they saw. Food, drink, plastic toys, photos, souvenirs, more food, more drinks, ice cream, pop corn, it never ended. Actors dressed as Disney characters mingled with the crowds, the heat must have been unbearable inside their suits. Anyone feeling the heat would have to hide behind the scenes before removing their costumes in order to stop kids from panicking. Imagine being a 5 year old seeing Goofy pull his own head off to take a swig from a diet coke bottle, yes, frightening, Goofy drinking diet coke when you had him down as a Budweiser guy.

We ambled around the park, walked around the lake and saw a few shows as we went along. Lunch was in one of the many restaurants on site and as we ate we were joined by Tara's favourite character, Tigger. I took a photo of the two of them together and Tara cried when he left.

"Are you OK?" I asked, limly.

"I think I'm missing our Little Man, I've always wanted to meet Tigger and I wish he'd been here with us to see him, to see this."

I was missing Jordan too, but knew he was in safe hands and being spoiled rotten by his Grandma.

We hung around the park until late in the evening. We saw the fireworks, the parade, and Tinkerbell sliding down from the top of the castle to the awaiting crowds below. There were gasps, there were cheers and applause and once again, tears. I didn't really get all the nostalgia for lost childhood innocence, I don't know I'd ever been innocent as a child or adult, I just felt it was a nice show, pretty lights, fireworks and actors, I didn't see Mickey and Minnie

Mouse, I saw costumes filled with hot sweaty actors on less than minimum wage, struggling to get through the day.

Trying to find our car on the way out was a nightmare. We knew it was a white car, couldn't remember the make, or licence plate, or where we'd parked. It was only by pressing the door button on the key and spotting the hazard lights coming on, that we found it at all.

Our next outing was Universal Studios. I hate rollercoasters and so avoid them at every opportunity. Thankfully there were many rides at this park that were designed for people like me, gentle moving floors and a lot of visual effects. I was very much in my element here, avoiding the fast rides and still having fun. Ever since I was a kid vomiting up my lunch after riding the rollercoaster at Margate, I'd never wanted to get on another one. I'd enjoy myself on the ground, going around and around on bumper cars or slow moving rides, The Whip, a spinning car with a foot control being the limit of my sensibilities at the fun fair. Being able to use the foot brake gave me a sense of control that made the whole experience bearable.

All was well until we were strapped in at The Alien interactive show, I thought something was actually behind me when the lights went out and a little jet of air breathed on the back of my neck. Was it the escaped Alien? No, but it did wake me up a bit.

The ET ride was gentle but still enough for me to wish I'd stayed at home. Tara grabbed my hand and began to run towards another ride.

"What's the hurry?" I demanded.

"Nothing, but the ride's starting in a minute and I know you're going to love it."

"What is it?"

"It's fine, you'll love it come on" she pulled me past the signs at the entrance to the ride. All I could read were the words Space and Adult.

"But isn't this a....?"

"It's only a ride, you'll be fine, it doesn't go fast or anything, it's in the dark, like a ghost train without the train-you'll love it!" There seemed to be a few too many "You'll love it's" for my liking and as I was dragged further up the ramp to the front of the queue I realised I was being hoodwinked. We had already passed the point of no return before I saw the sign describing my torture to come. It was Space Mountain, a roller coaster ride in pitch black darkness. I may have farted, once.....

"You'll be fine, it's in the dark, you'll love it!" Tara was starting to sound over the top with her reassurances, I was turning pale and weak.

"It's a roller coaster, I hate roller coasters, if I'm sick, you're clearing it up!"

We were strapped in, pulled forward and up a steep incline, I knew this was everything I hated but I also knew I had to endure it come what may, for the next 5 minutes of my life.

"Fuuuuuuuuuuuuuuuuu.........!" We tore away downhill, swerved to the left, right, up, down, around and around. I screamed like a little girl for the entire ride, my body relaxed because I couldn't see the bends and dips ahead, but my knuckles white and stomach somewhere nearer my throat than it should have been. I was not a happy bunny, I was about to be a violently sick bunny, an angry bunny ripping off the head of my wife bunny and slapping her with the wet end bunny, an 'if I die she dies' kind of bunny, the type that's never seen out of an orange jumpsuit kind of bunny.

"Don't ever do that to me again" I said climbing out the carriage, "I hate roller coasters."

"But I heard you screaming, you were loving it."

"I was not screaming, I don't scream" I lied, my face still grinning with a mix of relief and pride. The temptation to stab her in the head with a carrot slowly receded as the relief of terra firma beneath my pads filled me with reassurance. I had survived, barely.....

We hung around all evening and eventually saw the firework show, the big parade and Tinkerbell on a zip-wire. Tara cried and I drove home to the hotel wishing I was a 7 year old again, as an adult, the whole thing did nothing for me, and personally, I'd have preferred to have waited until Jordan was old enough to come along to experience this place, he'd have really enjoyed it, i just felt like I'd had my wallet picked.

Gatorworld was interesting, lots of powerful creatures clambering over each other to munch on dead chicken, their jaws powerfully snapping shut with the power to break a man's leg as they sink back beneath the surface of the water. The grisly Death-rolls beneath the surface designed to drown any animal in their grasp, and once dead, their body would be ripped apart, bashed on rocks and swallowed in huge chunks without any ketchup. It was like KFC on a school outing, nothing went to waste and very little was shared.

Once you've seen the dangers lurking beneath the surface in Floridian waters, there's no better way of passing an afternoon than taking a canoe ride along the bayou. A gentle paddle downstream, between the reeds, the low hanging trees and cobwebs. The gentle lapping of water against the canoe, and the eerie silence of the wilderness hanging in the air as we looked around at the wilderness. The thought of Manatees and Alligators watching us from below was always in our minds. So much so that when we came across a spider the size of dinner plate dangling at Tara's face level, she screamed and demanded we head back to the safety of our hotel. I hadn't heard any banjo's myself, but they were out there, somewhere, duelling in the woods….

Cape Canaveral lies on the coast between Miami and Jacksonville, but you know that anyway, just like you know it's the home of the Kennedy Space Centre, named after someone called Centre, weird bloke best left alone really. Home of the North American Space Agency, it is the site from where so many of mankind's adventures into space have started from. It is a place of enormous scale, where the biggest thing you've ever seen suddenly appears tiny in comparison to what is now about you. Nothing prepares you for just how big this place is. The launch pads, the Rockets, the vehicles, the buildings and hangars, everything is supersized and then some. I walk around in awe, every little boy dreams of going to space and this is the closest I'll ever get to it other than on the return flight home, peering out of the plane's window, down at the blue sea, and up into space. I'll never go where some of the hardware I saw at the Kennedy Space Centre had been, not in my lifetime, but I would have loved it, looking back at the Earth and away into the deep space that is unseeable from the surface of our home planet. I would love to see the multitude of stars that are blocked out by light pollution around me, I would love to feel weightless, to float as I had in the dreams of my childhood. I would love to be farther from home than I'd ever been before, only because I can, only because it's possible.

We toured around the site, our guide telling us all about the history, present and future of the space programme and the role Mr Centre had and will play in all of this. We entered the control room, the very place where all the action happened. There was a real sense of history, knowing this was the place where Gene Kranz heard the words that would have crushed a lesser man-
"Houston, we've had a problem here."

What exactly Whitney Houston was doing running around the control room at that time I don't know, but to hear those words, knowing it's on your watch, the whole world is watching and you have to bring your boys home alive, would have definitely spoiled your day. But not Gene, he was the Lead Flight Director of the Apollo 13 mission. He kept his cool, a "Pretty large bang" heard by the astronauts 55 hours into their mission was not going to ruffle his feathers. Instead, Kranz ordered that the planned moon landing be cancelled and the astronauts brought home-by looping around the moon, burning their thrusters and hopefully landing in the Pacific Ocean, not the Indian. It was bad enough that John Swigert had taken off without filing his tax returns, but for all three to drop into foreign waters without a visa or even a passport between them would have been highly embarrassing.

USA "Hello India, can we have our Astronauts back please?"

India "They're not Astronauts, the Earth is flat and sits upon the back of a giant Turtle, everyone knows that!"

 USA "But we need them back."

India "Then show us how to make good movies and you can have them."

 The Kennedy Space Centre truly is an amazing place, it's where dreams come true. People toil for hours, days, weeks on end just coming up with possibilities and solutions to things that they didn't even know were problems to start with. I've been trying to do that shit all my life and yet I still end up in the most ridiculous of situations. People who work at NASA are smart, not just clever, not just your average Geek on steroids, these people are like extra-terrestrial smart, for instance, if you wanted to send something to the Moon, you'd look up, aim and press the launch button. The guys in NASA aim it way off at a different angle knowing that by the time the object gets there, the moon will be there too. That's clever, like firing at a moving target, fire at where it is and you'll miss it, fire at where it's going and your projectile and target will both arrive at the same spot at the same time. But you have to know when and where that will be, which is why so many other space flights took place beforehand, they were all dummy runs to test the environment, the machines and the reactions of propelled vehicles to the Earth's Atmosphere and the brutal void beyond. I often wonder what really happened to the animals that were sent up into space and never came back. Did they make it to some other planet by total fluke, establish a colony of human hating Dogs or Monkeys? Or did they just slowly fade as the lights grew dim and eventually explode into a billion cells as the vacuum of space overwhelmed their ill-equipped space ship?

 Returning to our hotel room we got a phone call from a couple we'd met on the flight out. They'd booked a hotel nearer Kissimmee and returning home from Disneyland found their room had been burgled. Even the safe had been emptied. There was nothing we could do but be grateful it wasn't us, our honeymoon had not been spoiled, but it did make us worry a little more each time we went out.

Rosie O'Gradys Good Time Emporium was the turning point for me. I'd spent years in Junior School as a proud member of the Country Dancing Team. Hands on hips, forming lines, skipping to the music and all that jazz- been there, done that and at the time thought it was great fun (leave me alone, I was only 9 years old…) I had seen plenty of good old rootin' tootin' westerns in my time, and if I knew anything about cowboys it was they loved whiskey, dancin' and a darn good brawl to finish the evening. Nobody walked out of a saloon, everyone got thrown out the windows or head first into the horse trough, that was the law wasn't it? Anyway, there we were, looking across a dance floor at a row of people in line with each other copying every move, it was dancing by numbers, no rhythm, no sense of joy, stark, cold copycat motion. The clean boots, dust free shirts and denim all straight from a catalogue, nothing having ever experienced the dust of a trail, the nights under the stars, drinking from rivers, plates of beans and soggy saddles when you realise that that wasn't actually a fart. I felt a fraud watching this display, I felt sad that such a life was long lost in the past and anyway, weren't the cowboys the bad guys of North American History? I preferred the Indians, the Native American folk, they looked after the land, the animals, the resources. They killed and plundered too, every tribe, creed, race and Nation on Earth has crimes in its history, but the North American Story was written by the white men, the square dancing, belt holding, happy clapping copycats on the dance floor here. Soulless and uncaring. It was not what I had always looked up to. It was fake, a land of lies and falsehoods, cracking at the seams. The sooner we could get away from this money grabbing land of nothing for free, the better.

America had changed, it wasn't for the better, and I could sense the difference, there was a new normal coming, the future was going to be different, sober and somehow darker.

5 Rise

I am back in the cubicle, the small space that protects me. Light blue plastic veneer covered chipboard, the cold grey floor beneath the toilet is damp and frightening, hard and uncaring. My breath is short, shallow and at times too loud for my liking, it could give me away, it could reveal my whereabouts, that breath, held for as long as I dare. My heart beats loudly inside my chest as I lean forward to listen for it, the faceless, unseen thing outside the cubicle. The thing whose breath is able to flex the walls around me, that knows of my presence as it too leans against the manmade protective cage about me, listening for my heartbeat, for my breath. All the while, the tap drips, drip, drip, drip in its echoed threatening voice.

Life in leafy Buckinghamshire was exactly as it sounds, life in leafy Buckinghamshire. It was day after day of commuting to work, playing happy families and wondering what the fuck ever went wrong. It was the slow death of the soul. Repetitive, boring -it was everything this book and my life are not meant to be. The highlight of the normal week was Chicken Jalfrezi in an indian restaurant run by Bangladeshi's. It was death by a thousand yawns made tolerable only by the adventure of work.

I lost the job in Slough after not turning up for a shift on Christmas Eve, I was meant to be on call and the call came when I popped out to go to the local shop. When I got back I was told someone rang but there was no message.I called back but got no answer. I then got a letter a few days later calling me in for a disciplinary, where I was duly told my services were no longer required.

I found myself a job at Heathrow, working nights delivering Airfreight into the airport. Night after night of going from one agent to another, moving huge aluminium plates laden with freight, secured and sealed cargo carriers that rolled out the back of the trailer on a bed of air assisted rollers. The loading and unloading took moments, it was the queuing and waiting that took up my time. Each night I would spend so much time stuck in the driver's seat waiting, that I began to think I knew how a mushroom felt, alone on a piece of wood, in the middle of a forest growing older by the minute. The only bonus being the ear splitting take-off of Concord about 10pm each night, there was something special about that plane, the noise, the power and speed. Such a shame it came to it's tragic end in Paris.

Agency work followed and after a few days here and there, I was put on a long term position with a bed manufacturer famous for supplying the Royal Households, and yes, I did get to deliver new mattresses into Buckingham Palace, but you don't want to know about that, you don't want to picture me pulling up alongside the Palace with a trailer full of new mattresses for the most prestigious house in the world, you barely believed me when I told you I'd driven Prince Charles' car, so yes, the beds, I didn't even have to touch them. I pulled up and was told to wait, then drive in through the side gate only when instructed to do so. Once inside the Palace, I had to go to a glass cage and wait whilst the footmen of the house, wearing long black tail-coats and spotless white shirts and gloves, streamed out from another doorway and emptied the trailer without breaking into a sweat. Looking out from my transparent cell, I could see the occasional movement of a security guard on the roof or in the grounds nearby, this was obviously seen as a weak point in the estate, cameras were everywhere and one false move outside of the glass box (-I was told) would be enough to get me shot. But you don't want to know about that, do you? You're waiting for the Sex, drugs and Rock'n'roll to make a comeback, well trust me, so was I. But in the absence of all things immoral, illegal or just plain out of reach, I kept plodding on. I wrote poems and songs, hired a recording studio and got Tara and her best friend Lisa, to put down the vocals for a couple of my works. The end result was shit. The sort of bad pop song you get when you feel life is not your own anymore, and only Simon Cowell can produce music, where you watch too much Saturday night TV and your head is screaming for a beautiful, speedy death. Buckinghamshire was killing me. My only success had been a 5 minute TV show called "Your Shout", where I was chosen to represent my tarmac loving brethren, the Knights Of The Road, the Truckers all over the country who were getting abused by fellow road users for being in the way. The message was simple, "We're all trying to get somewhere in one piece, be patient, leave room for manoeuvre and stay safe." A removal truck was donated and I drove around the Industrial Estate in High Wycombe with a camera crew on board, then did the voiceovers in the back of a car, reading my lines as naturally as a long plank of Maple. I never did get that call from Hollywood, they must have rung after I moved away, story of my life really......

It was time to move on again. I knew it, Tara knew it, Pat knew it. Things were not 100% at home, our presence was having an impact on Pat's relationship with Stuart. We needed room to be a family too, and in more than just 1 room. Jordan was getting bigger and we needed a home of our own. I floated the idea of moving to the midlands, Coventry was not on the cards but Nottingham was. Being only a couple of hours up the

M40/M42/M1, an easy drive without having to change gear too often, we decided to check out house prices in the city. We found a house in Aspley, an area to the North of the city with easy access to the M1 motorway. The house seemed pretty big at first, well-compared to the bungalow we were living in with the In-laws and their ghosts it did. Every so often, for no reason, the house and garden would be filled with the smell of baking, the scent of hot fresh scones would fill our nostrils even though nobody was baking. Another good reason to move, if the ghost could bake scones, it could just as easily burn them and that wouldn't be good now would it?

Why Nottingham? I liked the idea of the history of the city, the fact that just about everyone in the world must have heard of it. Whenever I used to tell people around the world that I was from Coventry they'd invariably shrug their shoulders.

"Is it near London?"

"No! It's near Birmingham."

"Manchester, you like Manchester? Me like Manchester United" they'd smile. I hated football, but then they probably hated Punk Rock and people with tattoos and piercings too, so we were even. I thought if I lived in Nottingham at least we could talk about Robin Hood, or not.

Nottingham is famous for many things, men in green tights that lived in the forest being one. It is also famous for it's football teams, Notts County and Nottingham Forest. County Cricket and Ice Hockey rank highly too, not to mention the Horse racing at Southwell. An industrial city in the heart of the East Midlands, Nottingham had a huge lace making background. In more recent times Boots the Chemist had their headquarters based in Lenton. Raleigh bikes (remember Chopper's- just about everyone had or wanted one in the 1970's), and British Tobacco, Nottingham produced some of the most iconic cigarettes of the day, millions per day rolling out of the gates of their factory. But Nottingham was also famous for something else, it was home to Rock City, a venue I'd been to many times in my mis-spent yoof!

When we checked out house prices in the area, we also came across another statistic I'd never known before. Nottingham had a lively nightlife, something it was quite proud of and also encouraged, maybe because it has one of, if not THE oldest pub in the world, Ye Olde Trip To Jerusalem, and a population made of more women than men. Legend had it there were 5 women for every man in Nottingham, although sometimes that's quoted as 4:1. I have enough trouble when the ratio is 1:1 how the hell could anyone manage 5?

We bought a standard 2 up 2 down with upstairs bathroom and a garage which was huge, unfortunately, the access alongside the house was too narrow even for my tiny little Fiat Uno. Attempting to park in the garage meant a 10 minute exercise in breathing in tight, folding in the mirrors and staying straight all the way, the slightest deviation meant losing a mirror or scratching the bodywork on 1 or both sides. I eventually gave up and kept the car on the drive instead, it was so much easier. Not being the world's best gardener, I later dropped some plastic sheeting down and covered it with gravel, simple, useful but not very pretty to look at. We were quite lucky living where we did, our neighbours were ok on the whole. On one side we had a widow who kept herself quiet but was always happy to chat over the garden fence. On the other side lived a window cleaner and his family. These were not quite as quiet, there'd often be rows, they struggled with money and as we later found out, much of the reason for that was his addiction to alcohol and drugs. Sometimes he'd leave and stay with an ex-wife for a few days or weeks, then he'd be back playing happy families until the next crisis. The estate itself was an old council estate, it had a reputation for anti-social behaviour, car crime etc. This was mostly the fault of a few families from the neighbouring estate, Broxstowe, they were the quintessentially Chav Chavs, Council Housed And Violent, although Vulgar would have been a better term, it covers all labels at once. These were the families at the school gates in their dressing gowns and PJ's, too lazy to dress because their bit on the side was coming round once the old man was off to work.

I'd moved with the promise of work from a local branch of the agency I was working for in Buckinghamshire, however, once I arrived and called them to book an appointment there was nothing doing. I was out of work, with a mortgage and a family. I scoured the local rag and got another agency job almost immediately. This led me to a full time position working for a small family business, mostly collecting timber from the North East ports and delivering to a local Timber yard, not very glamorous but it just covered the bills. I'd been there for a few months when one of the planners told me his mate was in a band, and that I would probably really like them. He handed me a cassette one day.

"Here, have a listen, they're really good," he said. I looked at the label.

"Burdock, is that their name?"

"Yes, they've got a gig coming up soon in Matlock Bath, you should try and see them, they're looking for a new manager."

A gig, in a bath?

Really?

I played the tape on my way home and actually had to stop the car. I had not heard anything that good for many, many years. From the excellent belter of a song "Tom Said" to the exquisite "Typical Me" , the tape did not disappoint once. I wanted to hear more, I wanted to know who these guys were and when I could see them. I got home and made Tara listen too, she seemed to like them but wasn't as excited as I was, I had suddenly re-found my passion for new music, I wanted more, I wanted to get involved. I called the number on the tape and spoke to Ian, the singer.

"Hello mate, I was given a tape to listen to, it had your number on and I was impressed with what I heard, do you have any gigs coming up-I'd love to see you playing live?" I knew damned well they were playing, I just needed to find out when. Ian turned out to be a very talkative and likeable guy. We chatted for a while and by the time we hung up, he'd invited me to become the band's manager, Me-the manager of a band? I didn't even know what that meant, but I'd give it a go, once I'd seen them play live, maybe.

Matlock Bath turned out to be a town on the A6, not the swimming pool like I'd imagined it to be. Burdock were headlining a gig in a small venue beneath the huge rocks that made up the spectacular environment the town is set into. I arrived early enough to see the support act and hung around quietly at the back of the bar, in case they were shit and I could leave without anyone knowing I'd ever been there. I didn't know them, they didn't know me, nobody would be embarrassed and nobody would know we'd been in the room even. I was hoping for the best but feared disappointment, I mean why would they need a manager if they were any good-wouldn't they already have one? And why would they offer it to me, a truck driving song writing poet who'd never published anything other than a few trucking stories?

The DJ played his last track and introduced the band, this was it, Burdock, live in front of me and the whole room rocked, they were loud, fast, angry, soulful, tuneful and bloody brilliant, I loved it. They finished with an encore and I knew I had to introduce myself, I was hooked. Within a couple of weeks I'd drawn up contracts and had the band sign them. My membership of the British Academy Of Songwriters, Composers and Artists was finally paying off. I was the Manager of a band, and a bloody good one at that. I immediately set about trying to get gigs. I would call venues in London, Manchester, Liverpool.

"How many people will you be bringing with you?"

"There's me, the band and if I can get my mate to come along there'll be 6 of us." It was usually then that the phone would go dead on me.

"It's me again,I think we got cut off just now…" Click!

The other response would be to demand a guarantee, a deposit of £100-150 to play. Bands had to pay to play, who knew? I thought they turned up, played and collected the door money, with the venue earning their money from the drinks bought at the bar. But this was the end of the 20th Century, people had stopped drinking, they smoked weed and swallowed pills, they hung in bars for the atmosphere and the scene, but spent the night staring at their shoes, their dirty grubby tracksuits worn 24/7, their brains fried on ecstasy and skunk, too much dirty speed and heroin that was cheaper than guinness. I had no idea how bad the live scene had become. But I was finding out, fast.

I managed to get a slot at a venue in London, in Covent Garden. I hired a van and away we went. We arrived in time for the soundcheck and duly hung around as the support group played. A pretty naff, pretentious outfit with a frontman dressed in a red guardsman's jacket, he was lacklustre, unconvincing and the music was bland. There were a handful of people in the room, and when Burdock came on, there were still only a handful-including those in the support act who stayed on to watch. Where were the fans, the music press, the inquisitive? Had I not sent out dozens of texts and faxes, weren't they meant to be here clambering over each other to see this new supergroup? I needed to up my game, if the only response to the best band of the day, was the singer of the support act grudgingly admitting he'd been outclassed, then I needed to do more to get Burdock known and heard.

There was a Solar eclipse coming up and the whole country was excited at the prospect of a bit of nighttime at lunchtime. I wasn't too bothered but thought I'd try to see it if I could. As luck had it, I was in the Cotswolds and miraculously made it to the top of a hill overlooking the Vale of Gloucester. Hundreds of other people had congregated to watch it too, no matter how I tell myself otherwise-I was destined to be there. I had an empty trailer, I arrived in time to get the last parking space my truck could have fitted into, and just after I sat down the air went still. There was a calm wave washing over the entire environment, birds fell silent, traffic had stopped, people hushed and the moon passed between the Sun and the Earth. Some folk have described that moment as life-changing, the moment they found true peace, God or a host of other things. I just thought it was beautiful, sitting there on that hill as a dark shadow past over the land below and about us. For a brief moment it was nighttime, everything was still, eerie. It lasted only a minute or two, but it was enough to create a memory for all time, and then, as quick as it came, the dark gave in to light and the birdsong returned.

I changed jobs again, having noticed a local company with good looking trucks seemed to be everywhere I turned, I felt compelled to contact them.
"When can you start?"
I have to give a week's notice" I said.
"Excellent, so would you be able to go to Slovakia if we asked?"
"Yes, I've not been for a few years, but I can do that?"
I was taken on the following week and a week later was given a fax with the details of the trip to Slovakia.
"This isn't right," I said. "There's no way this will happen, that's not enough time to get there".
"Don't forget, you're going in a car with a little trailer on the back, no Tacho, no truck, you can drive a lot faster."
"I know that, but I'm saying we'll never get from Vienna to Zvolen in 4 hours, nor will we get to Vienna by lunchtime, who put this together, do they even know how far it is to Vienna?"
"The owner of the company sent this, you're going out with his man, you'll be the second driver and picking the boss up from Vienna airport when he lands." There was an implication that this was going to happen-wasn't it?
"I have no problems doing it, but there'll be no sleeping on the way, it's not been factored in."

As usual, I was right.

I arrived at work as planned and was taken by truck to rendezvous with Keith, the guy I was travelling out with. Sure enough, we had a Range Rover with a trailer on the back. No Tacho, but still legally required to keep to 60mph. Keith filled me in with the details. He worked for Mr Bance, the owner of Bance and Co Ltd, manufacturers of railway resting equipment. Our job was to deliver a track inspecting machine to Zvolen. The machine worked by sending x-rays into the rails and finding any tiny cracks in the steel. The machine we had was revolutionary as it could do so at much higher speeds than the industry norms, it could accurately read the rails in half the time of the machines currently in use in Slovakia. Our Mission was to get to Vienna and collect Mr Bance, then get to our hotel in Zvolen in time for a business supper with a group of both Government representatives and Slovakian Rail Authority bigwigs. The problem was, Keith couldn't drive the whole route, he'd recently had a triple heart by-pass and had so many tablets to take each day I was surprised he could ingest them all. It also meant he could get tired quickly and needed constant stimulation, I had to keep talking and guide him all the way there. We left his home in Mountsorrel, Leicestershire and headed south to Dover. We had to clear Customs on our way out, Slovakia was not yet a member of the EU free trade area, and Mike's plastic box with 150 different tablets in was a constant source of concern for me. He had a letter from his Doctor, but that was in English, I wondered how the Slovaks would react if they got shirty with us.

Keith didn't have a clue about the Customs procedures or the route to Vienna. He'd only ever dealt with companies in the UK and Ireland before, this was a new experience for him and a great opportunity for the company. This could be a fantastic opportunity to sell lots of machines. We were scheduled to do a presentation of the machines on a section of railroad the day after our arrival. Once finished, we could pack up and head back, Mr Bance would hang around and we could make a leisurely return home.

We were booked on the Hovercraft, a noisy craft that flew above the waves in calm weather, bounced through them when the wind blew and stayed ashore when it got rough-which was quite often in the English Channel. This was my first ever experience aboard the Hovercraft, I'd seen it riding up onto the beach and flying across the channel, but never been aboard, and having done it, I really didn't need to be repeating the experience. It was only a few months later that the service was operated for the last time.

We headed through France and Belgium to Germany and eventually arrived at Geiselwind around 10pm. We were both knackered, Keith especially.

"We'll have to set the alarm for 4am or we won't have a hope of making it to Vienna anytime tomorrow, let alone lunchtime" Keith was too tired to respond and duly fell asleep as soon as his head hit the pillow of his well worn bed in the hotel. 4am came around way too soon and we were back on the road straight after the first coffee of the day. I'd told Keith to keep his speed down once we got past Regensburg as there was a good chance of getting done for speeding on the approach to the border at Passau. He thought I was just a nervous passenger until an unmarked Police car pulled alongside us and the passenger showed me his badge.

"We're being pulled-" I said, "You'll have to get into the hard shoulder." The cops were polite enough, not too interested in what we were doing other than why we were going so fast. Keith was given a ticket and we were allowed to go, so long as we did so a little slower. I didn't want to say "Told you so" because the frustration in Keith's voice when he called the cops "Bastards" every other sentence, was obvious enough. His boss had screwed us over and all my predictions were coming true. Our lunchtime rendezvous at Vienna airport finally happened at nearer 4pm. Mr Bance had arrived around 12.30 and rang Keith's cell phone every 15 minutes or so thereafter. He was not a happy bunny and tried very hard to hide his own frustrations as he called Maria, his contact in Zvolen. I held my tongue as he made promise after promise.

"You'll have to meet them and we'll hopefully be there before dinner, you can start without us if you must and I will make the presentation afterwards." This eventually became "Keep them entertained until I get there and make sure they have lots of drinks."

Our ETA headed further and further into the late evening.Mr Banks' plan slowly looked as bad as I predicted. When we made the Slovakian Border it was my time to be in charge. I presented the ATA Carnet and supporting documentation to the Customs window. There were several grunts and something resembling a "For fuck's sake!" in Slovak. The grunter took the paperwork and stared at it nonplussed. He wasn't very happy. Everything was present and correct, I'd already checked it through before we left England, but this was the game, pretend there's a problem, something non-specific, then wait for the Marlboro, the whiskey or some cash to pass under the window to smooth the process. I wouldn't bribe him too soon, that was my role in the game, hold on, pay little and late. After a 15 minute wait, Mr Bance lost his cool and stormed up to the window.

"I demand to know what's going on, what is happening here? You, young man, do you know who I am-yes you? I am the Director of this company and you are holding up a very important event!"

I turned to Keith.

"This isn't going to end well…" The words had barely left my lips as the screen behind the window was pulled down. Nobody was going anywhere now. I walked over to Mr Bance and quietly explained that it may be best if he shut up and sat quietly with Keith while I tried to deal with the Customs Officers.

"This is outrageous, I have friends in the……."

"Shut up or we'll be here all bloody night" I intervened. Mr Bance looked shell shocked, had he heard me right, did I just dare to tell him to shut up? I had, much to Keith's delight judging by the barely stifled guffaw emanating from his lips. "Take him outside for a cigarette, I'll sort this."

I waited 5 minutes before returning to the window and pressing the bell on the desk. It was another 5 minutes before the blind was lifted. I apologized for what had happened and asked what the problem was, offering to put the error straight immediately. I interpreted the response as meaning we had to pay for photocopies of the attached documents, copies of which were included in the papers submitted. A small fee for this was paid and rubber stamps were banged onto the Carnet. The moustachioed customs officer pocketed the fee and then slid the papers back under the window before pulling his screen down. We were done, cleared to go. I walked outside and waved the Carnet at Mr Bance who was once again on his phone, pacing up and down the footpath. He was still promising to be at the supper, even though we would never make it, the Slovakian roads were not like those we had just travelled, they were less well built, maintained and lit, we had a long way still to go and time was short.

We bounced and bumped our way to Zvolen, finally arriving at our hotel around 9pm. By 10pm Keith and I were in the bar, Mr Bance had gone off to his meeting with the VIP group he should have been sharing supper with at 7pm. They would be well oiled by the time he arrived if Maria had done her job of keeping them entertained. Keith had just the one beer and went to bed, leaving me people watching in the bar as a disco began filling up, all the local bright young things getting jiggy with each other. Fatigue hit me after a couple of glasses of the strong brown beers I'd gambled on tasting nice, it was time to leave the locals to their strange gyrating and nocturnal fraternizing, time to get some rest before the morning show.

Mr Bance appeared at breakfast and was about as highly strung as I had seen him, the previous night's late arrival had not gone down too well with his potential clients. However, today was an opportunity for him to put things right, to demonstrate his invention. We followed the directions we'd been given and ended up at a rail siding a few miles away from the hotel. There was a group of dignitaries waiting and Mr Bance wasted no time in getting himself familiarised once again as Keith and I unloaded the machine onto the track. It was remote controlled, weighed about 100kgs in new money but thankfully was demountable otherwise I'd have broken my back getting it out of the trailer. Mr Bance took great pleasure in running the cart up and down the track whilst directing Keith to show the assembled group how the monitors in the trailer were picking up real time images of the interior of the track. I stood around haplessly smiling and nodding where necessary, feigning some sense of knowledge about the equipment, all the while Maria, Mr Bance's agent and saviour from the previous day, interpreted for everyone. There seemed to be a lot of police and security personnel around, I mentioned this to Keith and he told me that was because some of the people here were from various Government offices, some very high placed figures looking to spend a lot of money on this little cart. Our little demonstration went on for about 4 hours, then we were told that we could pack up and head back for home. Mr Bance would now continue negotiations and Maria would escort him to the airport at the end of proceedings. Keith and I were free to grab his pill box and rattle off into the sunset. I don't know if our demonstration was successful or not, did the Slovak Government and rail authority buy any of these carts? I never heard, but by the time I got home to Nottingham, I'd clocked up about 90 hours working and had a very nice paypacket waiting for me.

I hadn't been back to Coventry since my ill-fated return a couple of years earlier. Finding myself on a night out nearby one evening, I called H.

"The past is the past and long behind us now" he reassured me. I felt the same and never held anything against him. I'd missed having my best mate around, so when he told me that he was having a band practice that night and would I like to tag along, I jumped at the chance. In my absence, life had gone on for H. He'd learned to play guitar properly now and was in a band of his own as well as playing with Roddy Byers, the guitarist and songwriter from The Specials, someone he'd had been a massive fan of for years. He was living the dream now, and not only that but apparently, they were better than The Clash. We stopped at the off licence, grabbed a few cans and headed off to rehearsal. I don't know what had happened to The Clash in recent years, they'd split up a decade or more earlier, but if they'd become worse than The Old No.7 Band, then I really had been out of the loop for a long time.

It was great to see Helen and H again, there would always be a place in my heart for them, they'd been there for me many times and I was always treated like family. It felt as though a huge gulf had been filled, but in return nothing was quite the same. An underlying discomfort existed.

"He's turning into an alcoholic," Said Helen, "I don't know how to help him- what am I doing wrong Ribs?"

"Nothing as far as I can see, he's just living the dream he always had, he wanted to be a musician, be on stage, now he's living that dream, although it's not like he's Jimi Hendrix or anything, he's playing in a tuppence ha'penny band and his imagination is telling him it's the big time, let him have his moment, enjoy it while it lasts, but if the drinking is a big problem then it needs sorting out." I had no idea just how bad that problem really had become, nor how it would play out in the coming years. H had never been very good with drinking, he would get drunk too quickly, fall asleep, wake up and start again, to me it wasn't really an issue, he wasn't a nasty drunk, he never had a bad bone in his body, he just loved too much. It was to be another decade before he lost his fight with the bottle. I sat with him, his brother John and John's wife Edith, along with his friend Shan. We sat for 2 long days as he slowly slipped from this world on January 1st 2010 But that's another story, one for some other time and place.

6 Hobby For A Day

It's not that I never loved you

It's not that I never cared,

I just wanted everything

To have, to hold, to share

I settled in to the new job pretty well, mostly working around the UK at first. Once I had settled in I was given a regular truck to use, a Scania R113, and began doing regular trips out to Holland. We had an office in Tilburg, situated in part of the Gebruder Huybregts office and warehouse site on the outskirts of the city. We would handle all manner of groupage (mixed loads) in both directions. Sometimes full loads of Slimfast products coming back, sometimes full loads of printed packaging materials or Sturmey Archer bicycles going out. Some weeks I would go out once or maybe twice, some weeks I may do 3 trips if everything worked out okay, if it didn't I would be weekended in Tilburg. It wasn't the end of the world, that was just beyond the horizon, somewhere just out of sight. I became a regular on the Eurotunnel going out, a familiar face on the ferry from Europoort, Vlissingen and Zeebrugge. I was constantly on the go, changing currency and clocking up miles. I knew the Netherlands better than I did the UK at times, and Belgium too. Being on the road so much gave me the opportunity to meet other drivers, swap stories and pick up little bits of useless information. Much of this I would turn into words on the page and send to Trucking International for their My Mistake page. I would use pseudonyms and names of family members just to avoid always being the bad boy, I thought that if I used my own name too often, that future employers might remember me as the idiot who dropped a trailer on its knees, or drove into a farmyard and got shot at. There were many confessions on that page that would have been grounds for instant dismissal or a hearty guffaw around the office water cooler, some might even show one's ability to deal with any unfortunate incident, or just a prat having got into that situation.

Jordan was getting bigger and more and more inquisitive. We bought a Bearded Dragon and kept it in a vivarium in the living room. We'd often feed it together with a diet of Mealworms, Crickets and other tasty bites. Hand sanitizing was a must after handling him due to the risk of Salmonella on the Lizard's tongue. We also took in a rescue dog, Berty, he came from a kennel on the A52 and was very timid to begin with. Once he settled in, he became more loving and friendly but also more competitive around Jordan, there was room only for one baby in Berty's eyes, and that wasn't Jordan. They would both play happily together, but Berty would always be trying to take the role of the dominant male, he'd push Jordan aside, sometimes steal his food if he could, anything that he could not have gotten away with against adults. "Berty!.... Mum, tell Berty…" would be the rallying cry from the back garden or the living room. Whenever Jordan was playing, Berty would put himself between him and whatever toys Jordan was playing with. If Jordan got a hug, Berty would demand one, if Jordan got fed Berty would try to get his share. It was an ongoing battle between them.

Tara made friends with a neighbour around the corner, Gill. She would often pop around there for a chat and compare notes with her, both had young kids of a similar age and seeing as I was away a lot, it kept her company. Gill's husband was a relative- slightly removed, from the very famous cricketer Ian Botham. It wasn't long however before Gill and her other half parted company, the husband was dragged through the courts for maintenance and given Daddy-daycare privileges every other weekend. Tara spent more and more time with Gill and another friend, the three of them would often go on Girl's nights out into Nottingham and come home complaining (with a smile) about having been groped in the clubs and bars, many of which had reputations for being no more than meat markets for the sexually deprived males that tried so hard to disprove all theories of human evolution, Knuckle draggers in the highest order.

I'd written a story for Trucking International that was published in the same edition as a story about a British Truck Driver, Rick Hudson, who'd just been imprisoned in Macedonia. The war in the former Yugoslavia had been going on for a couple of years. British troops working for the United Nations were spread throughout the Balkans. Yugoslavia had self-destructed into a number of new countries, Slovenia, Bosnia-Herzegovena, Serbia, Croatia, Kosovo and Macedonia. British troops in Kosovo, part of the KFOR group of UN soldiers, were supplied via convoys heading from the UK via Italy and Greece, passing through (Former Yugoslav Republic of) Macedonia, which should not be at any time confused with the Greek region of Macedonia. A long court battle reigned in later years over the use of the name Macedonia, as Macedonians believed they were the only people who could call themselves Macedonians. The other Macedonians (*no,not those ones*) the (FYR) Macedonians (*them ones*), long held claim to the name Macedonia and eventually it was decided in court that Macedonia was Macedonia but Macedonia *(the other one)* was also Macedonia, whether the Macedonians in Macedonia liked it or not. Macedonians (*no not those ones*) were now Macedonians and the real Macedonians (*them ones*) were also Macedonians, just not the same. It was all very Greek to me, to a point.

Rick Hudson had been driving in a convoy of trucks and decided to take advantage of a clear spot on the road to overtake a vehicle in front of him, he pulled out and began to pass the other vehicle, ahead of him the road was clear and he kept going overtaking the truck beside him. Suddenly a car appeared on the horizon and was fast approaching, so fast that Rick had nowhere to go, he braked but the car flew straight past him and slammed into a tree at 170 KMH. There was no contact made with Rick's truck and the impact with the tree killed the 6 occupants of the car, as well as nearly waking up the goat that was sleeping in it's branches.. Rick was immediately arrested and taken to Skopje where he was given no legal assistance and thrown in jail for 10 years. When I read his story I wanted to do something to help. What I could do I had no idea, but I wanted to do something, I felt as though Rick had been left to his fate, nobody in Government, in Europe, or any of the Macedonia's wanted to help, it was not their business. Rick was held captive, a bargaining chip for Macedonia to bring to the table at a time best suited to its own plans and benefits. It seemed wrong to me, that a sober, professional driver could be imprisoned because of the actions of an intoxicated driver in another vehicle, driving dangerously and way too fast for the road and conditions. I contacted the magazine and was put in touch with the author, Rick's sister Frances, who put me in touch with an old school friend of Rick.

Phil had been best friends with Rick all through their school days, but they'd drifted and lost touch many years earlier. Phil had also read Frances' story and got back in touch to try to help free his old mate. Phil set up a fundraiser and spent a huge amount of time writing letters to people in positions who should have already had this sorted out. He told me how he'd contacted Eddie Stobart Ltd whose contract Rick was working on at the time. They'd managed to get his truck and trailer released by the Macedonian authorities within 2 days, but completely overlooked any assistance for the driver almost a year after the event itself. Rick was held in a squalid prison, he regularly witnessed people being beaten and tortured for confessions. His physical and mental health were suffering as a result, but his status as a KFOR contractor saved him from a similar fate. The thought of 10 years in this hellish place weighed heavily on him all the same. I joined the efforts and began sending letters to my own MP, to Downing Street, to Bruxelles. I wrote to magazines and told the story to everyone I met, trying to spread the word. I was invited to Rick's parents house, an elderly couple who lived in Derbyshire. We chatted about Rick, his upbringing, his family and the incident that led to his incarceration. There was no doubt, even in the evidence of the Court hearing, that Rick was innocent of any crime. He was a political prisoner, taken by opportunist means, to be used for political gain. In my eyes, Rick was a fellow truck driver who happened to be in the wrong place at the wrong time. It could so easily have been any of us, any driver unfortunate enough to be in his seat on that day. I offered to put on a concert, a fundraiser in Derby to raise money for the family to help with his substantial legal costs and the cost of getting food out to him, some of which he actually received, not quite everything was pilfered on route. Phil and I spoke regularly, he and Frances kept up the pressure as best they could. We all had our own jobs, family etc and Frances was living on a Spanish Island in the Mediteranean somewhere, it was a hard fight to get any real attention or support, I mean, let's face it, who loves a truck driver at the best of times, let alone one who's working in a contractually mercenary role in a warzone. His employer was a very small operator, subcontracted to Eddie Stobart who were themselves contracted to the British military, who in turn were operating under contract to KFOR in a UN peacekeeping role in a far off Balkan country nobody had heard of a few years previously. Everyone had someone to take the blame.

A venue was fixed and invites sent out. T-shirts were printed and sold with the slogan, Free Rick Hudson- It Could've Been You! It was the best I could come up with. I found a support act for Burdock, we found a caterer, and enough volunteers to make it all happen. Friends I knew in Coventry came over to work the door, set up equipment and tables, lights, PA and equipment. My mate Raoul did the door and at one point I found him in the reception with the local MEP pressed against the wall. Raoul was giving a lecture on how 'His Type' are only in position because people like us put them there and how he'd better remember it.

"It's alright Raoul, he's on our side!" I said rescuing the beleaguered official before he decided to use his diplomatic immunity to remove Raoul's pointy finger from his face.

Frances flew in for the event, family, friends, other drivers, the press, all turned out to hear Frances' pleas for help, her parents' own words and those of the local (now recovered) MEP. Representatives from Fair Trials Abroad attended and we raised a fair amount of money for the cause, mostly however, we kept the story alive.

I was in West Hallam, at a large warehousing depot run by TDG one day having brought in a load of Slim Fast milkshakes from Holland. On one of the other loading bays was a truck most drivers in the game knew very well. It was Chris Hooper's red and yellow Transcontinental. Chris was a well known owner-driver famed for his long trips from the UK to the Middle East, one of the last of a dying breed of Astran (Asia Transport) drivers. He'd recently had an article published in Trucking International of one his last trips to Doha in the United Arab Emirates. Chris was trucking royalty *(Yes, I did spell that right)*

"You alright mate, having problems?" I asked. Chris was under his truck, a cigarette stuck between his lips like a permanent fixture that never got lit.

"Got a broken leaf spring by the looks of it" he replied. He pulled himself back out from under the truck. Chris was a very experienced man, he knew the job inside out and I could only sense how much I still had to learn to be anywhere near his league. We chatted for a while and I told him about Rick and his plight. Some of the Middle East boys had already heard of what happened in Macedonia, not only that, but they were willing to help.

"If you can get him out of prison, we can get him home" he promised, placing a £10 note in my hand. It was to be a few more months before any good news came through.

Phil called me one day.

"I've just been told" he said in a conspiratorial tone, "nothing written in stone, but they're saying Rick could be home for christmas." I wasn't ready for this. "That's brilliant news mate." I said unconvincingly, having half expected to hear the exact opposite, that he'd been given an extra term to serve. "We can't let the press know, nothing can get out or they might just change their minds, everything's happening behind the scenes, private meetings, no press coverage, no embarrassing headlines for Skopje…" Was it really true, was Rick actually getting out, so soon, and so quietly, why, was it the gig? Rick was finally released on December 23rd and flown home to be with his family for christmas. Between christmas and New Year he came to visit me at home, to thank me for my help and being in touch with his family. I felt very humbled to see him here, in my living room, on my sofa, thanking me for having helped release him. I felt I'd not really done much, I had done something, I did what I could, which was better than nothing and in doing so,

I had helped another human being in ways I have still never to this day fully appreciated. Rick was free, he was home, safe and reunited with his family. I had never been to Skopje, I never saw his reality, but I felt his gratitude in the words and tears we shared. We had been strangers until this moment, but now we were friends, yet were destined to be strangers again, our lives would continue as they had done before, Rick needed to be home with his family right now, recovering from his ordeal, and I needed to be with mine.

"You should've been here yesterday" Said the Dutchman loading my trailer. "Why, what happened yesterday?" I asked. I was loading at a Pharmaceutical warehouse in Oss, Holland. Making small talk with the lad that was to load my trailer, I had told him of a story I'd written for the magazine and he now had one to tell me, one that would open my eyes and capture my intrigue.

"My best mate was here yesterday, we were friends at school together" he explained, as if I was meant to know who his best mate was. *(And no I didn't)*

"Uh-huh?" I asked politely, somewhat unsure where we were heading.

"Yes, he's on his way to Moscow now. He has a wagon and drag, does three trips and buys a new truck again." Nothing spectacular here, lots of people were going to Moscow at this time, and a whole lot further too, except me.

"Three trips to Moscow?" I asked, disbelievingly and a little bit jealousy.

"No," he smiled, "Three trips to Japan. He's on his way to Japan." he laughed.

"He does what? Japan, how?"I had heard that people like this existed, but never yet come so close to meeting one. If only I'd been there the day before.

"He loads here for Japan, the load is perishable, hazardous aerosols and have to go by road, they can't go by plane and the ships are too slow, so he drives to Vladivostok and gets a ferry to Japan. He loves it, you should go with him and write a story,take pictures of him all the way to Japan- make him famous." I would have done exactly that had I not missed him and had a mortgage to pay. His story certainly needed to be told but I couldn't justify a 6 month journey to write an article worth only a few hundred pounds, no matter how much I wanted to. I had already read tales of people driving trucks from Prato, Italy, overland to New York in the USA. They'd driven across the frozen sea at the Bering Straits, crossing from the farthest point of Siberia into Alaska and down through Canada into the USA. These epic journeys were the stuff of legend and excitement to me, I loved the idea of going farther and farther, the discoveries, the trials and successes let alone the sense of achievement at the end, to reach the destination against all the odds, that was survival, endurance and dedication. I'd read books by Ffyona Campbell who'd walked around the globe, I'd read The Cola Cowboys, the early Middle East truck driver's pioneering the routes now taken for granted. I'd tried unsuccessfully to become an expedition driver before going to Israel,I'd read of Scott of the Antarctic, Shackleton's Endurance, and yet I still hankered for my own expedition, my own drive beyond the horizon, my own story of success or failure, regardless the outcome, I was willing to try. My passport was riddled with beautifully coloured stamps and visas, from the border at Schirnding, to Medvedov, Hegyeshalom, Rajka, Bulgaria, Turkey, Israel, Jordan and the USA. There were empty pages awaiting to be filled with the evidence of a life well lived, travel and adventure still to be discovered. There are few people who understand this need to wander, this desire for expedition. Most people desire security, routine and safety, being home in familiar surroundings, some of us find we have a desire for more, a yearning for travel and adventure.

It was about this time that I found out about a festival at Morecambe in Lancashire. Holidays In The Sun was a weekend event and hosted a whole load of Punk bands in one big venue. I'd never been before and wasn't too interested until I found out that Cock Sparrer were headlining. I'd never seen them, but I remembered they were a band Andy Nunn had loved. I liked them musically but was wary of the political nature of many of their supporters, I decided I would pop along for the night driving from Nottingham to Morecambe on the day and hung around in the venue. Bands came and went, some I recognised, some I didn't but there was something missing, this wasn't what we were about. Punk Rock by the seaside, a weekend of band after band going through the motions. A generation of youth culture turned into product, beer swilling, walking product. I knew now exactly what Crass meant when they said Punk Is Dead, because this was not Punk, this was not the scene I had known and loved all my life, it was replacing the Rock 'n' Roll weekends that the Teddy Boys of the 1970's held, the very things we were meant to be usurping, where was the change and uprising we'd demanded, where was the passion, anger and rebellion? This was a holiday camp, controlled purchasing of merchandise, fashionista's puking up pints of cider in the street, an army of leather and studs, organised consumerism for the "Anarchists" of the day. The only redeeming feature was an excellent show from Cock Sparrer at the end of the night. It had been billed as their last ever UK performance, but it wasn't, they played again the following year, several times, and I missed them all. My time with Punk Rock seemed limited now. I have still never yet returned to the "Rebellion" festivals, the bands are often tempting, the occasion, less so. It's not that I feel in any way above or beyond, I just feel detached from that which I was once a part of, I have moved on, I have changed and find my attention and passions elsewhere now, I feel no attraction to the uniform, the compliance of non-conformity, following the rules of the game. I live in a world I no longer control, I follow routines and systems I don't always agree with, but I do so for my own benefit. I have the world at my fingertips, I can come and go as I please, I fit in, anonymous, free.I saw the world had moved on, that Punk was irrelevant now, it was a passing phase that had been raped and bastardized by the very establishment that now controlled it. It was part of the mainstream, our fashion of necessity (ripped, dirty clothes that we lived in week after week) was now being sold in boutiques, heroin chic was all the rage, high street shops sold torn clothing at rip-off prices, I hated it. Punk Rock was nothing more than a product.

Being a regular traveller to Europe had it's plus sides. I would buy packets of sweets in Belgium and Holland that I couldn't find in the UK, not for me, for Jordan. He got the candy piggie faces and I got cases of Amstel beer, not a bad deal at all really. The night boat from Europoort, Rotterdam put on a good feed too. The drivers would all gather at the bar eating olives and fresh Rollmops, swigging pints of fizzy lager and out-doing each other on this week's shenanigans. No matter how bad your week was, someone else had it worse. I got to know a few regulars including one fellow who owned a flower shop. Every week he took his 10 ton truck out and came back with a fresh load, same route, same suppliers, same old, same old. One Friday night his son was on board instead. Someone enquired about the old fellow

."Dad had to retire, he rang me last week, he said he didn't know where he was and I had to talk him back to the ferry, he's not coming back."

That was it, decades of running the same same route had taken its toll, I knew how it felt to momentarily feel "Where am I?" after being lost in my own thoughts, but this was long term, this was serious and I didn't like the sound of it. The thought of being somewhere so frequently and not recognising it, knowing you know where you are but you don't because your mind and memory are gone. It seemed like the loneliest place in the world, somewhere I didn't want to go but one day I may have no choice in the matter. It can happen to any of us.

Burdock had recorded a new album and I did all I could with my limited experience and contacts to get it out into the outside world. I sent copies to radio shows, DJ's and music reviewers. In return, we got nothing. The whole industry was a closed door affair and apart from a handful of pub gigs, there was little I could do for the band. I decided it was time to move on and I resigned my management of the band. I would still support them, attend gigs etc, I just felt that my position was probably hampering them from getting a real manager and record deal. My time with the band had been fun, but I could do no more for them, it was time to go our separate ways.

I saw an ad in the local paper, someone was putting together a group of young boys, singers and dancers, a Boy Band. The ad had stood out to me, I knew that the universe was trying to tell me something and so I called the number given.

"Hi, I'm calling about your ad, I'm a songwriter, I don't sing or dance and I'm too old to be in your troupe, but if you want any original material, I may be able to help you."

"I have a dance studio in Lenton, come and see me Monday evening, about 7pm."

The spiel had worked, I was in.

Monday evening I turned up at the Dance Studio just as a group of under 8 year olds were finishing up and their parents collecting their prized little ones stood proudly in the reception.

"Are you Ribs? Come with me." Diane was petite, in an underfed, overstressed kind of way. In our conversations, she would go on to tell me she was separated from her husband, almost divorced. A single parent she was struggling to make everything work, the home, the studio, the dance classes, everything was hard work and having me offer to help was a godsend.

"I want them to be up there, like Boyzone and all them, they can do it, they've got the moves and I'm working on the harmonies, but the songs-we need new songs, original stuff. Do you know any studio's-where we can record, do you know anyone?" She bombarded me with questions and explanations for things I'd never asked, but overall, I got the impression she was trying hard and against all the odds was just about coping. I also got the impression that she liked me. I didn't know any studio's but did some hunting around and found one. It was newly opened and called Nightbreed. I made the arrangements and a couple of weeks later turned up for the recording session of a song I'd written called "New Millenium."

I was greeted by a guy with long black hair, Trevor. Our paths would cross again in later years, but he probably doesn't remember, or maybe he's too polite to say. I remember it well, he wore black head to toe, and despite his best endeavours, was unable to hide his displeasure at recording such drivel. The vocals were lame, the lyrics ok, and the music was like nothing he'd normally work with. Trevor was a Goth, he also liked some Deathrock and Metal. I felt like he was talking another language, what was this stuff? There were only ever 2 kinds of music in my day, Punk and Rock, everything else was just hearsay. Goth had come from Punk, it captured the dark theatrical side of the genre, bands like Killing Joke, Siouxsie And The Banshees, UK Decay had all been punk bands that were easily labelled Goth. Alien Sex Fiend and Specimen were the true sound of Goth, along with Bauhaus and Joy Division, The Cure and Sisters Of Mercy. When I'd been a regular gig and club goer in the early 1980's, I knew and saw most of these bands, but I had totally missed the whole Goth thing. Goths were just posh punks in make-up with classier looking girlfriends. I had missed an entire generation of youth culture, I knew nothing about any of this stuff.

Trevor recorded the song to the best of his abilities considering he hated Boy Bands and pop drivel, which was what I had brought him.

"How soon will the track be ready? We have a gig coming up soon, a launch party for the song."

"I'll get it back to you in about a week, is that ok?"

"Yes mate, that'll be plenty of time."

I was very impressed with the finished item, 2 tracks, 1 with and 1 without vocals, just the backing track to use when performing live. Diane and I both thought it was good enough and that the boys would do a great job with it.

All we had to do now was invite the audience and members of the music press, local papers etc. We were going to make it work.

The night came around very quickly. There'd been only 2 or 3 rehearsals between the recording session and the show itself. Diane had managed to get a local nightclub to let her use the venue for the launch of the song. It turned out that the lads had done us proud and the place was very busy, filled with proud Mums, sisters,aunts and cousins, all that was missing was the Industry. As the zero hour approached, I took Tara upstairs to the balcony, ostensibly to get a better view, but in reality to hide away from everyone.

Diane took to the stage and thanked everyone for coming and then introduced the song.

"And I especially want to thank our songwriter, the man who made this possible……" *(A huge part of me died right there and then.)* "Where are you? Can anyone see-oh there you are, up there look, thank you so much for writing this lovely……." *Still dying, slowly, painfully…..Make it stop… I may be smiling but….*

And then it started, or at least, it would have done if there had been an intro. We had overlooked the most important part of the backing track, the intro. Because the music and vocals began simultaneously, we should have had a metronome or drum beat or something to count the song in. 1-2-3- and…. Instead, there was a pregnant pause, the boys all looked at each other, I looked at the DJ, the DJ looked bored, Diane looked at me and then the music started the boys came in late, their voices out of synch, their movements out of time and the whole building cringed for a moment. By the time they hit the second verse they'd all caught up and the Mums and the Sisters and the Cousins and the milkman were all dancing, their arms in the air, wiggling their jiggy bits, everyone was happy, except me. I got out of the club at the earliest moment as soon as the applause was over. I had tried to find a vehicle for my songs, a way of making my words come to life but failed miserably. I was embarrassed by what I'd created and my connection to the boys, to Diane, to the Dance club were over. This was not who I was. These were not my people. My people were out there, somewhere away from this.

I found one of them soon enough. The circles of the universe that bring us all together, the 6 points of separation from everyone on the planet. It's real. I placed my basket of shopping on the counter and started packing as the young lady passed me my scanned items. She was slim, attractive in an alternative way, and there was something about her I recognised, not personally, but inside. She half smiled at my small talk and then mentioned a band I knew of.

"You should go to Rock City sometime, they have some good club nights there and lots of gigs" She said.

"I haven't been to Rock City in years, not since I was living in Coventry and we used to come over."

"999 are playing soon, supporting Iron Monkey, it's their last ever gig. You're from Coventry, do you know Paul from Raggity Anne? We grew up together in Scarborough." I didn't know Paul, but I'd heard of him, I knew his name from years earlier but never met him, not knowingly at least.

"No, I've been away from things for years now, and I was over in Israel for a year and lost touch with everything, are there any good bands around now?"

"There's loads, there's been a resurgence of punk bands, mostly from the west coast of the states, you must've heard of…." and began to reel off a list of names I had never heard of. It seemed that between my spending years overseas driving trucks and drunk fighting with soldiers in the middle east, I had totally missed out on the music scene. I had been left behind.

"Here-" she said, passing me a cassette. "My name's Meka, you can have this, have a listen to it, there's some good stuff on that." I took the cassette and thanked her, I said I'd hopefully see her again and left the store.

I had never heard most of the bands on that cassette, but suddenly I needed to. There was a mix of brilliant tracks, some of which became my new favourite songs, songs like Edina by Rancid, I loved the dual vocals, clever lyrics, so bloody catchy I had to ask myself why I'd not listened to them before, I'd known of this band since 1987 when Acide, the almost toothless street punk from Montpellier had told me about them, but I'd never checked them out. There were others too, The Hives, The Von Bondies, Reverend Horton Heat. I felt that the world had moved on and left me behind, I'd lost an entire generation worth of fantastic music. I'd taken a different path and the price had been paid, being on the road and out of the country for years, never knowing any of the new bands that had been entertaining crowds in my absence. There was so much to learn and no time to do it, instead, all I could do was catch up as best I could. In my teens we were treated to the wonder of MTV, now I was finding P- Rock TV, MTV for kids with spiky mohawks and tartan pants. The music was good but what was all this skateboarding and cycling malarkey?

The gig at Rock City came around soon enough. 999 put on a blinding show to a minimal audience, a half filled venue with barely a handful of people who even knew who they were. The little room to the far side of the main venue was packed by the time the headliners came on. I was close to the front for the show, the last ever gig Iron Monkey would play. I'd never heard them, knew nothing about them except they were big with the local crowd. They played a heavy mix of doom and metal, not my thing, but they were good. The whole venue erupting with each new song, the heat almost unbearable created a mini environment where sweat rose to the low ceiling, condensed and fell in bitter tasting droplets. I'd never been in a venue where it was so hot it rained inside, it was unbelievable but thoroughly worth the ticket price.

It was coming up to the end of the year, decade,century and Millenium.. 1999 was turning into 2000, and with it came not only the threat of the Millenium

Bug, a predicted meltdown worldwide as computer systems failed to register the change of date at Midnight on 31st December 1999. Fridges, cars and microwaves were expected to stop working, Tv's were predicted to go blank and aircraft were meant to fall like rain from the skies. It never happened. Instead, we got a particularly nasty winter flu bug instead. Tara managed to get Bronchitic Pneumonia and as poorly as I was, I drove her to the doctors picking up a puncture as we arrived, not only that, but the glass in the drivers' window fell down into the door interior, the outside temperature was low enough to turn nipples to coat hooks as I struggled to get the car back into a roadworthy condition before Tara came out from her consultation. We coughed and sputtered our way home, and spent the rest of our New Year's Eve prostrate on the sofa.

I had not fully recovered by the time I was due back at work. I loaded the car up the night before, as I always did, but when I came down the next morning the rear offside window was smashed and the case holding my work clothes had been stolen. The 21st century had arrived without a bang, just a foretaste of the shitstorm to come.

Gill moved to Birmingham leaving Tara a little lost without her friend around the corner. Jordan started school and then abruptly stopped. He was a smart kid and didn't fit in at the local school, neither did his mother. She'd turn up at the school gates fully clothed, wearing her own knickers, her hair done and make-up on. The majority of the other mums would be sporting dressing gowns and PJ's, no knickers but pink furry slippers-even in the rain, chain smoking and talking badly about the bastard fathers of their bastard sons, the fucking this and the fucking that, poxy fucking bastard life on the dole with only the Lottery to look forward to when there's no heroin left on the estate. If ever a family did not fit in with their surroundings, it was us. Nottingham had never felt like home, not that I actually stayed there much myself, I was up the road more than I was home and it was starting to take a toll on all of us.

Tara began home-schooling Jordan and he seemed to thrive, not just on the attention and 1 to 1 tuition, but on not having to mix with kids with whom he didn't mix with outside of school. He was a very smart child, and sensitive too but always smiled and loved to laugh, play and learn. Like most boys, he loved Dinosaurs and was pretty much addicted to Godzilla, Jumanji and Beetlejuice. He loved nature programmes, anything to do with animals and wildlife, the bigger the better, Walking With Dinosaurs was almost constantly on the TV and Jordan knew everyone of them by name, to the point he even declared he wanted to be a Paleontologist when he grew up, which I guessed wouldn't be too long.

I came across an advert in a local newspaper. Someone was putting together an anthology of poems for young writers and I submitted something Jordan had written, a poem called The Future.

The Future

The time capsule landed 50 years in the Future,

There is enough data for robots to exist.

I look so strange, wrinkly, ugly and much older.

More people are coal miners, there are more car factory

Mechanics and a lot less cars.

People are not allowed to believe in religion,

They could be put in jail.

I am having more and more nightmares, I'm in the middle

Of a war and cities are being bombed.

I look inside the factories and all I see is military

Equipment being made.

More soldiers are securing towns, villages, cities and

The White House.

To me war is horrible!

Anyone caught playing football will be executed.

Bombings are so popular that every town, village and

City has an air raid siren.

Schools do not exist.

People are very shy, they carry gas masks.

After the bombings lots of people are killed in their houses.

It is now the end of the war, everything is back to normal.

Food is scarce, there are lots of famous people but what

Will the future hold?

I don't know.

Jordan Reid.

7 Warhead

Twisted bodies, flesh and bone
Screwed up corpses with no homes
Entrails and bodies for all to see
How in death your heart shall bleed.

"There's a burning sun, and it sets in the western world, but it rises in the east and pretty soon it's gonna burn your temples down…." *UK Subs- Warhead.* No lyric could ever have been more fitting. Everybody alive knew where they were when they heard the news. I was in Shrewsbury, or at least very nearby. I'd stopped for my lunch break, having pulled into a layby at the side of the road bursting for a piss, got down from my truck and relieved myself into the hedge. As I was finishing off I heard a strange noise, and for once-it wasn't me farting. I shook off the dribbly bits and put my crown jewels back inside my pants, carefully tucking the wet end into the top of my ankle sock *(think about it, take as long as you need…)* There was something in the hedge, something other than the former contents of my bladder. I leaned in and with my arm outstretched was able to grab an old, rotting piece of rolled up carpet. I pulled it back out and sure enough, found the cause of the noise. A litter of kittens had been dumped inside the rolled up carpet, thrown into the hedge. There was nothing I could do myself, other than put the kittens into a cardboard box and then look for help. A jogger was approaching and I called her over. She was an older lady and had connections with both the RSPCA and a local newspaper. I couldn't have found a better person to help.

"You'll get a mention for this!" She said.

"Detention-for what? I didn't do anything!" I thought I was back in school. The lady took full control of the situation and had an RSPCA van arrive in a matter of minutes. The kittens were taken away and I was assured again of being mentioned for my heroic discovery in the local newspaper in a day or two. I can just imagine the headline- *Hero Trucker urinates on Kittens!*

I drove away from the layby and the news came over the radio, an aircraft had crashed into the World Trade Centre in New York. Until only a few years earlier, I knew nothing about this place, even though I'd seen and paid little attention to the twin towers when I was being shown around New York by Marybeth in 1987 after leaving France.

"It's the World Trade Centre, do you want to go to the top? It's like 3,000 storeys high or something"

I thought about it for a second, did I want to go to the top of one of the biggest buildings in the world,? *(second only to the Empire State Building.)*

"No I think we'll give it a miss today, I'm not in the mood for heights."

It wasn't a lie, I really didn't fancy shooting skyward at a rate of knots only to look out at a vomit inducing height above the city, it really didn't appeal to me. I was still of the belief that the Empire State Building was the tallest in the world. The Burj Khalifa hadn't entered my radar at this time, and even when my later wife Nikki brought home photo's of the twin towers, I still hadn't clicked that they were taller than the Empire State Building, they couldn't be. As far as I was concerned they were pretty big, but unless King Kong was going to be re-worked and have a twin climb up the other tower, I was not changing my belief to suit any modern narrative. The Empire State Building was still the tallest in the world, end of.

The reports were a little confused at first, it was assumed it was a light aircraft, some rich idiot having lost his way in the sky and missed the last invisible exit back down to Newark or somewhere. Possibly an engine or rudder malfunction, no reports of any casualties, to begin with. Then the story began to grow. It wasn't a light aircraft, it was a passenger jet. Was it foggy in

New York, had the pilot not seen the towers? Speculation was rampant as the reports came in thick and fast. It was definitely a passenger jet and it had crashed into one of the towers. Casualties numbers were going to be high. My phone rang, it was Tara.

"Have you heard the news?" She asked.

"Yes, I was listening to it just now, some sort of accident, a passenger jet crashed into a building in New York."

Tara was watching it on the TV news channel. The BBC had some footage of the event they kept showing, it was just the building with smoke and flames pouring out of it.

"God, it's awful" She said,"those poor people."

I couldn't see the images, and to me it was just an accident, a computer malfunction or tired/drunk/dead at the controls pilot, probably not a good day for him to quit smoking, or drinking. I've seen the film Airplane enough times to know what really goes on in an airplane, they don't call it a cockpit for nothing and those inflatable auto-pilots, woah, steady on.

I had no idea what happened inside the World Trade Centre, but in the next few hours I- and the rest of the world, were about to find out.

"They're saying on the radio that a lot of people must have died and been hurt, what's happening-has the plane crashed to the ground or what?"

"There is no plane, it's just gone-like totally vanished, there's just a great big hole in the building and flames, there's things falling out of the hole, papers and stuff."

"That sounds pretty bad, anyways, I'm heading back now so I should be home-"

"OH MY GOD!" Tara almost burst my eardrum. "There's another one!"

"Another one? Another what?"

There was silence on the line, just the muffled background noise coming from the TV set Tara was watching.

"There's another plane crashed, just now, another one, I just saw it!"

"What?" One plane crash I could understand, but another into the same building seemed a little far fetched. "What d'you mean another, are they repeating the footage or what?"

"No, oh my god, I just saw it, another plane crashed into the other tower." The urgency, confusion and fear was evident in her voice. Whatever she was watching was really scaring her, this was not a drill, no mistakes, something terrible was happening and I could do nothing. I had no idea of what was really happening, only the images I could conjure in my own mind. The big blue sky over New York City now the scene of a major incident. The radio kept updating with the latest news that could be gathered. Tara called me again, and then again and again. There was a hijacking, no, there were two or more. The President of the USA, George W Bush was rushing to hide somewhere, the US Air Force were threatening to shoot down other aircraft.

There'd been an explosion at The Pentagon, the whole of America was in a state of panic. My thoughts turned to all the people I'd known and loved in America. The friends I'd met in Israel, Chuck, Tree *(-although she was actually Canadian)*, Rachel *(-so was she)* Steve *(yep, he was American)* did any of them work in New York? I thought of Mark Gazda, could he have been there? What about Deana and her Mum, what about Marybeth? What about Alex, Jerry…? My mind was racing in circles trying to keep up with the news that was coming in. Trying to picture the scene being described in that city. New York was being evacuated, what the fuck? War had broken out without warning and nobody, but nobody, had expected it. This was Pearl Harbour for the modern day, a stealth attack right into the heart of the biggest power in the world, someone had been sleeping at their job and now they were paying the price for it. No matter what I did, I could not get rid of my thoughts for those I knew in America. I genuinely feared that someone I knew would or could have been there, on a plane or in the towers.

"We are just getting reports that one of the towers of the World Trade Centre has collapsed."

Tara called me back for the 213th time.

"It's gone, the building collapsed-it's just fallen straight down into itself" She was in shock, this traumatic event was playing out live on the radio and visually on TV screens the world over. We were not prepared for this. Nobody had ever foreseen such horror to ever play out live on TV. Phone lines to New York were down. The Pentagon was in flames. Planes were being diverted all over the world. America was at war but nobody knew who with.

"I can't believe what I'm watching, people are jumping out of the windows of the tower."

I'd heard this on the radio. People were seen falling from the sky, crashing onto the canopy of the building a lifetime below them, people jumping to a certain death instead of burning alive in their offices. I couldn't imagine the horrors that were playing out, I could only listen to the reports and take each new horror as it came. I wished I could call Deana, Marybeth, Mark, Chuck, someone, anyone. I felt as though I was being attacked, that the people I'd known and loved needed me now, they could be there now, they could be dying, burning in the remaining tower or falling through the sky. My biggest fear had always been falling from heights, that stupid, useless time when you try to swim through the air only to crash into the ground at a hundred miles an hour. The thought of willingly jumping from a window 100 floors above the ground only to crash into the steel and asphalt canopy, to have to choose to do that because where you are right now is so much worse, how fucking terrifying is that? How can it be that jumping is the better option? How terrified must those people be already. The unimaginable horror.

"NOOOOOOO!!" Tara screamed again. "The other tower, it's fallen as well, both towers are gone." I could barely take in the enormity of everything that was happening. Without a visual aid, all I had were vague memories and an old photo to go by. I had to wait until I got home to be able to see the reality of the horror that I'd heard unravelling that day. There was nothing I could do but wait until I got home. The radio updated itself minute after minute with all the changing news and commentary. Nobody knew who the attackers were to begin with, but bit by bit news filtered out that the Hijackers must have been part of a group and the whole thing had been coordinated, planned many months in advance.

When I finally made it home I could barely remove myself from the sofa in front of the TV. The images being re-run, again and again, the narrative of the witnesses was truly harrowing. I knew now what it must have felt like when Orson Welles first broadcast War Of The Worlds to an unsuspecting nation, people took to the streets to fight off the invaders from Space, they honestly believed it was happening and were reacting accordingly, the difference here being this time it wasn't fiction, it was real. The world was suddenly different. Nothing felt safe or certain, there was a palpable fear in the air, the sense that war was coming and that it would be a very different world from now on.

I had heard again and again on the radio every moment revisited, from when the first airplane struck, to the moment when the second tower collapsed. It was truly the most traumatic experience I have ever known. Nothing before or since has had the same effect. The world stopped still, momentarily silenced, stunned and confused. Millions of people the world over were horrified but unable to stop watching, listening to every word, every update. 9-11 was now the most infamous day in modern history, a true life horror that traumatised a generation.

I followed the news for as long as I could stay awake, day after day. The world had changed and it no longer felt safe and secure, the world was fluid, scary and so much more dangerous than it had been so very shortly before. People were scared and visibly traumatised. When news came through that people in Palestine were celebrating, there was a lot of anger in the West, a lot of hate boiled up and anyone with brown skin was suddenly deemed to be The Enemy. The true perpetrators were soon discovered to be members of a Middle eastern terror group called Al Qaeda, an extremist Muslim group who's sole raison d'etre was the destruction of the West.

I won't go into the whys and wherefores, the history books have plenty of text about 9/11 and all that followed. For the sake of brevity and to stop anyone else closing this book before the end of this chapter, with or without a bookmark, I shall limit coverage of the subject, except to say that for younger people who weren't around at this time, you must try to understand how different a world we enjoyed before this awful date. When I say the world changed overnight, I was not exaggerating, it really did. Suddenly, 'Security' was the new norm, the new buzzword, everything had to be assessed for security, airports, Borders, Trains, Busses, the very fabric of the free world was under strict scrutiny.

It wasn't long before the full extent of the attacks and the carnage they left behind, became apparent, within days the enemy was named and a massive military machine set about seeking revenge. Thousands of young men and women volunteered for action, signing their lives away for a chance to pay something back, to kill in the name of the fallen. An eye for an eye plus interest charged. Death was woken from his slumber and took full advantage of the situation, laying waste to hundreds, then thousands and tens of thousands of human lives.

At work we began to deal with more and more military contracts, I was sent one day to a Military base in Lincolnshire to collect a load of Rockets destined for Turkey. The word on the grapevine was that 'Our lads' were going into Afghanistan. Speaking to one of the soldiers who loaded my trailer, the contents of which I was not allowed to see, I asked if this was true.

"We're flying out to Turkey and then into Iraq, but that's not our final destination, can't say where, but we're going very soon."

"You might need this-" I said, handing the soldier my Qafir, the black and white headscarf I'd bought from a Palestinian Arab in Bethlehem a few years earlier. "Tie it around your face to keep the sand and the heat out while you're over there."

My gift was graciously received and I headed off site to take my trailer to a military dock in the south of England. Travelling down the M1 an hour or so later, I was amused to hear Foreign Secretary, Jack Straw talking on Radio 4.

"We have No plans for military action in Afghanistan, we will not be going to Afghanistan, our focus is solely in Iraq."

I looked at my mobile phone sitting teasingly on the dashboard, already mapping out the conversation in my head.

"So Mr Straw, we're not going to Afghanistan-no? If this is the case should I just turn around right now and take these rockets back to the base where I loaded this morning-I mean, it might save a few thousand in taxpayers money if they're not shipped out for a wasted journey."

The devil on my left shoulder said *"Do it, go on, show the fucker up!"*

The sane voice on my right shoulder told me I would probably disappear and never be heard from again if I did. I looked at the motorway in front of me, feeling like I was part of some small group of people who were *'In the know!'*

The devil on my left shoulder leaned in to whisper *"Chickenshit!"*

The world was in a state of flux, there was change and insecurity everywhere, including in Nottingham. Our move up the M40/42 a couple of years earlier had been a good thing for us in some ways, we were able to buy a place of our own and make some new friends, but the distance from High Wycombe was just a little too much. Tara was feeling detached from her family and with Gill moving to Coleshill and then Birmingham, she was feeling a little distanced from everybody she knew.

"We can't afford to move to Wycombe, the house prices are stupid down there, but if you wanted to, we could go halfway, see if we can find a place near Coventry." I put the ball in Tara's court, knowing that in truth, it was pretty much the only option on the table. I knew I could get work around Cov and maybe build some bridges, get back something of the social life I was desperately lacking in Nottingham.

We found a house in Keresley Village, on the northern outskirts of the city, it was an old mining town, long since redundant and hopeless in it's psyche. We were not to know this, not yet anyway. All that we knew was that we liked the house, it seemed a nice area and the value of our home in Nottingham had almost doubled in the few short years we'd lived there. It seemed like the universe was telling us to sell up and go.

When the time came I gave a week's notice at work and took the week off as holiday, If my boss had not been such a dick I would have given more notice, but when you're treated like a number, played against everyone else and your job manipulated to only ever benefit the company, you don't feel like being considerate in return.

Moving also meant some other changes. When we acquired Bertie from the RSPCA, part of the deal was that we couldn't move him out of the area, something I still can't work out to this day. I mean, it's not like he had any family he visited in the area, he didn't spend time at the local Dogs Working Men's Club, or go to the football every Saturday. I could understand if he did, but Bertie was a home loving dog who wanted nothing more than a good feed, a play in the yard, run around the block and to occasionally hump my leg, even though I doubt he knew why he was doing it, he was that daft. So unfortunately for Bertie, he couldn't come with us, nor could Elmo, our Bearded Dragon. I sold him and his vivarium to a family in Boston. He just about survived the journey there, Coventry would have been too far for him without his heat lamps.

On the day of our move the removal truck arrived nice and early. The house was packed and wrapped, stacked and stuffed into the back of the small truck. Our entire life's possessions in the back of a 30ft Pantechnicon removal truck, everything except our computer and stereo, I thought it safer that we put those in the boot of our car just in case we never saw the truck again. We waved off the removal guys and locked the house for the very last time. There were no tears, no regrets or insecurities, the future was happening in real time, a whole new adventure was under way. A new home, another new job, even though it was with the company I'd worked for before I left for Israel. They were willing to give me a second chance and I was looking forward to seeing some of the old team again. I had a feeling Mark would welcome me back, even though we stitched him up so brilliantly at the works' christmas meal a few years earlier when a client in London had been harassing him about a very urgent delivery, Mark had kept taking his calls and apologizing, then when he wasn't expecting it, I got a friend he didn't know to call him and pretend to be the client, he was so worried he didn't realise that we were all stood behind him at his table until we tapped his shoulder. He had a sense of humour and took it so well, even though he did call us all a bunch of bastards at the time.

 Two minutes after leaving the house, we were waiting for the traffic to clear at a roundabout just before the motorway at Junction 26. I saw a gap and went to go but another car sped into view and I braked, I looked for another gap but it was too late, there was a violent shove and we were launched forward. The driver of the car behind had not expected us to stop and ploughed into the back end of my car, crushing the boot and pushing us into the flow of traffic on the roundabout.

"Shit!" Screamed Tara. I hit the brakes and managed to turn the car enough to stop any further collisions.

"Are you ok?" I looked across at her, then into the back seat to check on Jordan. Both were fine, although the shock was enough to make Jordan cry. I got out of the car and checked the damage before making sure the other driver was also uninjured. It was a young woman driver, she too was crying and upset. When she saw Jordan in the back of the car she was even more upset. Somehow I managed to get her details from her and called for my insurance company to assist with a tow truck. Before long everything was sorted and with the help of her father, an insurance salesman for the NFU, we were on our way to the new house in the back of his big white Jaguar. I really could not have wished to be rear ended by a better person, and if I could remember her name,I would highly recommend that you all pull up in front of that young lady at a roundabout, somewhere, sometime, especially if you've never ridden in a Jaguar before.

 Coventry once again welcomed me with open arms. The warmth and friendships of the people I had first met back in 1982 remained unchanged. There were some ghosts, some bridges that needed mending and since Nikki had moved out of the city, it was my time to put things right. I would never be rid of the guilt of leaving my daughters, but I was back with a son and a new wife, one who would not drag me down with her insecurities and tantrums like Nikki had, Tara was a stronger character, she was far more in control and able to lay down the law.

 Having spent most of the last 4 years or so away from home, I was looking forward to starting some local work, actually getting to go home more than once a week. I was sent to work from a warehouse in Magna Park, Lutterworth. The company had grown and now ran a contract to distribute to all the PC World shops in the UK, we did a few other shops like Office World and other distributors too, but our main job was with the Dixons Group outlets, carrying hundreds of thousands of pounds worth of computer and electronic supplies. These were the sort of loads that made you look in your mirrors a little more often, just to be sure you weren't being followed, loads like these were highly desirable and easily sold on.

We settled well into our new home. It was a beautiful little house full of antiques and character. Lots of dark wood throughout and the kitchen was like something from a Country Living magazine, with old biscuit tins on the shelves, copper pots dangling from a lazyboy above the little dining table. In the living room I had my collection of antique books on shelves around the tops of the walls, There was another shelf full of 'Crinoline Lady' decorated chinaware, taking prime position was a dark wood cabinet full of beautiful objects we'd collected from car boot sales and Antique Fairs around the country. The previous owners, a mixed race couple who adored Jordan and left him a room full of lead soldiers, Golliwogs and other vintage/antique toys. They had done an amazing job of looking after the place, not only that, but Jackie became a close friend, we would often bump into them at car boot sales around the area whenever her husband wasn't working at the London Taxi Manufacturing plant in the city.

Jordan started at the local school and was doing incredibly well, the problems experienced in Nottingham were behind him and he flourished in class. In due course, Tara was invited to become a Teaching Assistant and eventually went on to help out in reception. Things were going well for us- which is never a good sign,and so there was only one way for things to go, downhill.

Things at work had been good and I was pretty happy with everything, but changes began to come in. We started getting new contracts into the warehouse on top of what we were doing, there was a lot of chatter about what was happening and it was all bullshit, it always is. If you want to know what's happening ask the drivers, they know everything, because out in their trucks they hear every word that is spoken in the boardroom, in the transport office, the HR desk, everywhere, you can't open a drawer without a truck drivers' ears falling out of the gap. Things came to a head one day and I lost my rag when I got back to the warehouse. The actual incident was pretty petty and I overacted, hard to believe-I know, but when I get to that point where I feel I'm done then it's time to walk. I knew something was up, but I couldn't for the life of me put my finger on it. The things being done at the warehouse in Lutterworth didn't make sense. I couldn't believe that this was what Mark wanted us to do, he wasn't like that, and the organisation seemed to be going to shit, we were wasting so much time and money it was almost criminal. After blowing my top at my supervisor in the office at Lutterworth, I drove to the head office and asked to see Mark. He'd been good to me and I didn't want to let him down, even though I was.

"Mark's not here at the minute, can I help you?" Mark's number 2 was an affable guy, a bit younger than myself I thought, but he'd been with Mark from the very early days and worked his way up as the business grew.

"Something isn't right over there mate, I don't know what it is, but something doesn't make sense and I can't sit by and be part of it anymore. Can I transfer back here?"

"Well what's going on-what d'you think's going on?" There was a clue there, right there, a big fucking clue that went right over my stupid bloody head.

"I don't know, I can't get my head round it but it seems like everything's running deliberately at a loss, like it's meant to fail and I can't see why anyone would want it to, maybe I just don't get it, but I just can't work there like this."

Number 2 looked at me a little relieved.

"I'm afraid there's no vacancies here, if you can't go back to Lutterworth, then there's no work for you."

I was not going to win this, and something in the air said it was time to go. I didn't get to see Mark again, my time here was done which was sad, I wasn't happy about this, it wasn't how things were meant to be. I found out a couple of years later, that was the last day Number 2 worked as well. Unknown to me, a plot had been running in the background and the plotters had set up a rival company in a bid to usurp the company Mark had spent so many years building. I was told they'd got upset that there was not a pay rise but yet Mark had just bought himself half a million pounds worth of gardening services at his big new house. For some reason this was enough to spark a rebellion, an attempt to destroy the one company and divert all the work to the new business. I may have been a bastard stitching Mark up in the pub years before, but I was not the sort of bastard that would stab him in the back in such a treacherous plot.

I'd been considering having a vasectomy for a while and decided that maybe it was about time I actually did something about it. Tara agreed it was a good idea and so all the necessary preparations were done. On the day of the operation, Jackie drove us to the hospital in Nuneaton. Tara didn't drive and I was not going to be in a fit state to drive home afterwards. We were shown to a private room where I was instructed to get changed into a dressing gown and await the surgeon. I sat on the bed as Tara and Jackie made some smalltalk. Then the door opened.

"Good morning, I will be your surgeon today, my name is Doctor……… Now, which one of you is the patient?"

Forgive me for my naivety, but as I was the only person in the room with a set of testes and definitely NOT obviously a woman, AND that the operation booked was to be a Vasectomy- the removal of a Man's ability to reproduce, I thought the answer was blindingly obvious. All of a sudden my faith in the NHS, and this single Doctor in particular, was brought into question. Although, with hindsight, I can imagine him dining out on this story forevermore. *"You should have seen the look on his face!"*

We came out of a club in Hillfields one night, Tara, myself, Helen and H. I think we'd been to see Stiff Little Fingers, but it may have been PiL or Killing

Joke, although, I really don't have any memory of the gig whoever it was. As we walked past the mobile burger van heading towards The Swanswell, someone caught H's attention and suddenly the atmosphere changed.

"Do you know who I am?" Demanded H, he was now fully upright and his chest puffed up. It struck me that the lad H was talking to, obviously had no idea of who he was, nor was he bothered, impressed or concerned. A little voice in the back of my head said *"This won't end well."*

I turned to help my friend as he attempted to use his height and social standing to impress an obviously impressionable youngster. He hadn't come to grips with the notion that people who don't know you have no respect for your ego, the younger generation were faster, more apt to hit and run or look for your weak spot while you're still arguing the point in hand, by which point they are already three punches ahead. Our generation survived by grandstanding, blagging our way for the most part, we were not as sprightly, we were not like pack animals circling and testing, we puffed up our chests and sounded indignant. H had already lost this fight and I knew it. I stepped forward just as he took the first punch and fell backwards. I grabbed for one lad but immediately felt myself dragged sideways. Punches came in thick and fast, I had 3 of them on me, a fourth kicked out at the prone body of my friend, unconscious on the floor. I lashed out where I could and managed to grab hold of someone's throat, my balance was rocky and I knew I was going down soon as the punches kept coming. There was a small wooden rail just below knee height behind me, I was being forced backwards and was in danger of getting a total hiding, if I could get one of them out of the game I would have a better chance with the other 2. My fingers dug deep into the guys throat and I pulled and twisted my body at the same time as we went over the rail. I had managed to turn him round and he landed on his back cushioning my fall as I continued to strangle him. His eyes were pleading as I squeezed harder and tried to get up off the ground, someone was on my back and then boom, a kick to the side of my head momentarily knocked me out, I fell sideways, limp and useless. I was stunned but not defeated. Determined not to take any more of a beating on the floor, I shot up and almost drunkenly threw my arms about. The guy who'd taken H out had been busy as I fought his friends, removing H's mobile phone and wallet from his pocket. The group were already running from the scene, I followed for about 20 yards before turning back for my mate who was just coming round. Helen and Tara were screaming for help, my head was dizzy and my vision blurred, but we were both alive and well, bruised and bloodied, but at least now, those young lads knew who we were, eh?

8 Dominion

Dreams are like gateways, the entrance to our fears and loves, that which we run from and that which we crave. The demons of my slumber are many, some easier to define than others. Transported back to my childhood, to the corridors and bathrooms of a time long lost, my restless mind relives the fears of those innocent times. The fear of my cowardice, of wishing to flee through endless corridors even as the contents of my bowel escapes me. The fear of facing up to that unseen entity in the stall next to me, or behind the door. The beast that chases me, relentlessly at my heel, is not some fearsome reptile, no fire breathing spectre from hell, it is no phantom, no ghastly beast, it is I, the mirror image of myself. I am running from my own desire, my success and stability, the person I could and would be should I actually make it through this life. It is my success that scares me, because failure is the easy option.

I looked into the face of the old man in front of me, he didn't understand what I was saying to him, so I decided to try one more time, if he didn't get it then, I would have to find someone else to ask. I chose my words carefully. "Next year, are there many drivers in Poland who would come to England to work? To come here, to drive and live?"
The old man's face broke into a warm smile and he visibly relaxed.
"Yes, many driver want come to England."
"So if I make an agency, you can send me drivers?"
"Yes, but you must speak my son, my son speak good english."
We were sitting in the drivers' restaurant on an Irish Ferries ship, making the now regular crossing from Pembroke Dock to Rosslare. I had a new job and had for a while now been playing with an idea. We were a year away from giving freedom of movement for millions of workers in Eastern Europe. Workers from Poland, Hungary, Romania and Bulgaria as well as the Baltic states and some from The Balkans, would be allowed to live and work freely in the EU. I had realised early on that this would have an effect on the European job market, especially in the UK. Suddenly millions of new workers would hit the market and force wage rates to fall. If unscrupulous employers were left with a free rein, they would exploit this to the full. Wages, workers' rights and employment rights could all take a nosedive. I could see what may happen if nothing was done to stop this. These workers needed protecting, and so did the European workforce, neither should be exploited because of

the sudden expansion of the Union. I was toying with the idea of setting up an agency, bringing in the labour that was coming regardless, but ensuring that each and every driver would be paid the same rates as their European counterparts. When a driver in the EU could earn £400 per week was suddenly to compete with a driver from Bulgaria on £200 a month then it was obvious where the captains of industry would send their HR personnel. There was a serious risk that our livelihood was under threat.

Waldek was an employee of Pekaes, the Polish state carrier, a company with thousands of drivers on the road. If I could tap into this market, I could be part of the solution and reduce the risk of the industry being sold out to the lowest common denominator. I took the phone number he offered me and promised to call his son Tomasz. For the rest of the sailing, I had a new friend and was treated warmly by Waldek and all the other Polish drivers on board, each of whom I was personally introduced to.

When we docked in Rosslare, I placed the paper with Tomasz's phone number into my phone book. Waldek would be home in a week's time and talk to him before I make my call. With all this in place, I fired up my Iveco Stralis and headed up the country to Athlone, in the Irish Midlands, a run I would sometimes do up to 3 times a week, unless I was going into Europe. It was hard work, and anyone who's driven in Ireland will agree that a lot of the roads were less than ideal for speeding trucks. The main transit route to Athlone from Rosslare was nothing more than a narrow track at its worst point, and some of the potholes were big enough to cause havoc. It wasn't too long ago that one of the drivers from our company, Coventry Express Services, had hit a pothole in the face of an oncoming container truck, the resulting collision cost him his life.

Back home in Coventry I called Tomasz. Waldek had prepped him and we spoke at length about my idea to set up an agency. I had never run an employment agency and other than the occasional stretch here and there, my times with agencies were only ever brief. This didn't deter me from wanting to do this, I was sure that it was for the best and was willing to learn on the hoof. Tomasz understood the situation perfectly and said that he thought it was a great idea, he would gather together the names and details of all those drivers that were interested in what we intended to do and run the Polish side of the operation. I'd leave it with him, he'd call me back in a couple of weeks. I returned to work, excited at the thought of this idea actually coming to life. It was to be a couple more weeks before I heard from Tomasz. He sent me a text message that read- "Sorry I have not called, my Father was killed in an accident." I immediately replied that I would wait and he should concentrate on looking after his family right now. "Thank You" came the reply.

Waldek had left to return to work the week after he got home, he worked away for 6 weeks and then had a week at home. He'd overtaken a truck in his car, travelling at 160/kph, there was snow on the ground and conditions were less than ideal. In the opposite direction, another truck pulled out to overtake a slow moving truck laden with timber. Waldek died at the scene. Tomasz later told me about his father's funeral. After the service, the family returned home for drinks and food. The telephone rang and Tom's mother answered the call. There was nobody on the line, just the hiss of white noise through the receiver, she looked perplexed and hung up the phone. Tom called a number to identify the last caller's telephone number, it was Waldek's mobile phone. Tara and I had long discussed the idea of setting up the agency, in turn she'd spoken to her mother, Pat, who'd spoken to her new partner, a businessman who worked for a huge multinational company. He was very well placed and had contacts in very high places, he was a self-made millionaire and very impressed by our project. So much so, that he thought we should be able to make millions of pounds out of it once we were established. I was keen on Pat coming on board, because I thought that between her and Tara, the office side of the business should be well covered, as much as this was my baby, I needed help to do things that were not in my realm of expertise, like computers. I had no idea how one worked, how you'd connect to the internet, how to set up a website, how to do just about anything. I thought a spreadsheet was something that went on your bed, that a floppy disk was a freebie that came with Smash Hits magazine back in the late 1970's. I had a lot to learn but I thought I was in good company, that they were a way ahead of me in these matters. Pat and Tara could go out and talk to potential clients, win us the work we needed to get guys out on the road. Tom was good to his word and in a few weeks time he'd amassed a dossier with 500 drivers' details. I couldn't believe it, so many people wanting to come and join us, so many people willing to leave their secure jobs to come and start again. I'd never been to Poland but decided it was time this should change. I needed to draw up contracts and get things set up properly, establish a real business with Companies House and the Tax man. Things were taking off, big time. I had agreed to rent an office space upstairs in the building where CES was based, I could continue to work and use the weekends to establish the business. The space in question was just an empty space. Stuart *(Pat's now ex-partner)* came to the rescue. He and I built an office with stud walls and a complete new floor and ceiling. Just as it was all coming together a chance meeting with Gill from the office next door, opened up a new opportunity. Gill *(not that one)* ran an agency, GB Recruitment and supplied staff to the company H worked for. It really is a small world. Gill's partner had left the business and she was looking to sell up. Pat acquired the business for £5K and now we were running. The acquisition was a mixed blessing, it would give Tara and Pat the experience needed to get our business going and work as a shoe-in to the industry. As good as this was, it also created a barrier. Tara and Pat were running before they could walk. It was decided they would go to Poland to see Tom, collect his contacts and discuss the future. I stayed home with Jordan, the women bought new suits and matching soft briefcases. When they returned, there was little change, the contracts we needed to draw up for clients and staff were still nonexistent. Everytime I brought up the subject, I was sidestepped, there was always something getting in the way. I proposed we went away somewhere quiet together to sit down and work it all out.

We rented a farmhouse in Brittany for a week and I began to relax. Time was running out, we needed to get these things done. Pat and Tara's trip to Olsztyn had achieved nothing in my eyes. Sure, they'd built up a relationship with Tom and his family, but none of the important issues had been worked on, rates of pay, holidays, etc etc. It was falling on me to work out the fine details, not exactly my speciality, but I knew these were all important things that needed careful attention, and soon.

We arrived in France, to a beautiful rustic farmhouse in a small village miles from any major conurbation. Perfect. On Day 1 we went shopping. We found a local supermarket and stocked up on our bread, butter and jams, sausages, ham, and wine. Everything we'd need to lock ourselves away and work on the contracts, once we'd been to the beach.

Day 2 we headed off to the beach and ate out at a restaurant on the promenade. The weather was fine and with it not being the tourist season, the roads were nice and clear. Everything was going well, if only were there on holiday and not business, it would've been so much nicer to relax and enjoy.

Day 3 we headed to another beach and walked around a marina, looking at all the lovely boats, it was beautiful and if we had only been there on holiday and not business, it would have been so much nicer to relax and enjoy.

Day 4 we headed to the beach and when we went back to the house, I flipped. "We have to get this sorted, we're meant to be drawing up contracts, not running around having a nice holiday...." My words fell on deaf ears and I could not see a good outcome. "Look, this is my baby and I am very passionate about it, but I cannot carry on like this, I will help you all I can, I will advise you all I can, I will do whatever it takes, but I can't do this, I can't. You can have the bloody business, I am not interested in running it when you don't want me to be part of it and won't listen to what I say. My knowledge of the industry seems to mean nothing to you. So take it, do it your way, do what you want, I'm done....."

I picked up a bottle of wine and stepped out into the evening air. I was done. They could have it all now, it was all they wanted, handbags and gold jewellery. They loved the idea, power dressing all week long but not knowing how to work a fax machine. This was the point where I knew it was over, the writing was on the wall now, we were on borrowed time. Once home, I bumped into Gill in the corridor at work.

"How's it going? Is everything working out ok?" I asked. "Not really, they haven't got a clue, they're spending all day staring at empty screens, nobody's picking up the phones and being proactive, I don't know how they intend to manage when I finish next month!"

The writing was most definitely on the wall. The clues were there alright, Tara dancing in the kitchen to Michael Jackson songs pretty much put paid to our love life, confirmation came when she was using the computer in our spare room one evening. I was watching P-Rock TV in the lounge. 24 Hours of Punk/Ska/grunge music videos. The best thing to happen to TV since MTV.

"I'm just getting my credit card" she informed me, rummaging her handbag. "What do you need that for?" "I'm signing up to friends reunited, Gill says it's fun, I just want to have a laugh online, nothing else."

"I don't think that's a very good idea, I really don't think you should be doing that, it's not a good idea." Tara smiled and carried on regardless.

It was only a few days later that we met in the kitchen and Tara asked outright. "Are you Happy- I mean, really happy"

Now this is one of those questions that can have two answers or one answer, dependant on the person asking the question, their motive. It could so easily be a trap leading to guilt ridden regrets, or it could be a genuine question asked by a proper grown-up.

"No!" I gambled, "Not really."

I was ready for the fireworks, the screaming and crying, the slap round the face and all that was to come, but it didn't. Instead, Tara looked into my eyes. "Me neither, what should we do?"

"Well, I don't know, I mean there's no point fighting or arguing over stuff, we don't have to fall out over this, especially in front of Little Man."

We hugged each other like the grown up's we were trying to be, both shed a few tears as we discussed what we might do now. I decided I would move out of the house, I didn't want to upset Jordan any more than necessary, I would leave them the house and everything in it, see if I could move in with Brophy. I was now free again to continue my Yachtmaster training, something I'd been wanting to do for as long as we'd been back in the UK. I contacted the UKSA in Cowes and booked myself onto a mile-building course, something to refresh my skills before going on to chase my dream, Yachtmaster (Ocean) with Professional endorsement, the key to a career at sea, my route back to Eilat and the life I had loved and missed so much.

In the meantime I still had to work. It was coming up to christmas and I got that phone call, the one where you know someone's up to something but you're not sure what exactly.

"How many days does it take to get to Madrid and back?"

"Well that depends, if you were loaded and left from the yard, you can get there, with a local reload - full load, same day and straight back, 5 days -IF everything goes ok and there's no hold ups anywhere."

And so it was, the week before christmas week I got the reply.

"You're doing locals on Monday for the Jag, then Tuesday you're going to Madrid and reloading in Madrid, then home christmas eve."

I had a feeling this was not the case, but I went along anyway. Monday was spent collecting parts around the West Midlands and running the loaded trailer into Land Rover at West Bromwich. When I got in on Tuesday, my paperwork was on my seat. The load was yet to be collected from Stoke on Trent, then shipping out of Portsmouth that night. I was up against it already and had to plot the rest of the trip out very carefully, every minute counted as to whether I would be home or not for christmas. I drove up to Stoke and spent 3 hours on a loading bay as the trailer was filled with boxes full of sports clothing, destined for a supplier in the centre of Madrid. I hadn't been to Spain for a while so this was a bonus for me, in a way. I got the ferry overnight from Portsmouth to Caen, then drove hell for leather to the South. I made it past Bordeaux and stopped overnight at a service area near the forest. Next day I made it past Burgos and down towards Madrid. I got into the city the following morning and spent 4 hours unloading outside a sports shop on a narrow street in the very heart of the city. Once I was empty I headed out to a groupage warehouse near the airport and reloaded. Time was not on my side and I knew I was not getting home, but I could get into England and then get a train or bus home if needed. I ran hard for the border and drove every minute on the clock. I was booked on the very last Ferry out of Caen on Christmas Eve, as I pulled into the dock I had an hour to spare. "Can I park my truck in the dock in Portsmouth? I'm out of time and can't get home?" I put on my best begging face, but it wasn't enough. "No, I'm afraid there's no parking allowed in Portsmouth, you'll have to park outside somewhere. It's company policy, no parking over the holiday. What would you like to do, you can park here over the holiday."
I booked myself on to the next crossing, on Boxing day, returned to my truck and watched as the other late arrivals pulled into the dock, ran to the booking office and boarded the ship. Then I sat and watched as the ferry sailed away, without me. On christmas morning, there were another 8 trucks parked alongside, all of whom had missed the boat. As it was Christmas Day, the last Ferry to arrive overnight was disembarked and then prepared for the ship's company and their family's to celebrate aboard. A member of the crew brought plates of food down to the drivers on the dock. We were invited on board for drinks and I cheekily asked if we could go on a tour behind the scenes to see the bridge. To my surprise we were, and an officer took us behind the closed doors into parts of the ship we'd never normally have access to. The Bridge, the Control room and even the engine room. Until you see for yourself the size of a ship's engine, you can never fully understand just how big it is, and how much work goes into making it work, constantly.
I moved in with Brophy and Tick soon after. Brophy was busy on the road touring and living the dream as roadcrew Tick worked with him and when he was home would spend most of his time asleep in his room. Most days I had the house to myself, which was great, when I was there.

H asked me if I could do him a favour one day, he wanted me to sit with him as he went through Detox. He wanted to quit drinking and needed someone to stay with him for a week. I agreed and put in a request for a holiday at work. The request was denied and I had to let him down at the last minute. The reason for the denial was that I'd already been booked to go on a European tour. Instead of taking care of my friend, I was shipped off to Bologna, Italy with an exhibition load for the annual Book Festival. From there I was sent to Munich to collect a load on behalf of Nokia. It was a new product they were releasing and we were to take the promotional display split between 2 trucks, my own and Darren's, another of our drivers who I met with in Munich. We left Munich together and drove North to Stockholm, Sweden. Once there we had to await instructions and eventually unloaded at the main train station. The promotion team set up the exhibit and spent the next 5 days selling and promoting the new product while Darren and I went off and got drunk. Very drunk. We stumbled upon a party boat in the marina, a ship called The Pauline and began chatting to a couple of girls from Finland who lived and worked in Stockholm. They invited us to stay at their apartment if we wanted to, although it was a no strings arrangement, we were not to get any strange ideas. We were guests and the girls were not interested in any hanky-panky. This suited me fine, I was not really interested in anything else at this point. The ship had 3 decks each with a dancefloor of its own. I decided to head for the bar on another deck and as I was climbing the stairs I said something to a woman coming down the other way.

"You are English? Oh my god-I've never kissed an Englishman before!" I had no choice but to fulfill her wish and tick that box for her, and so we kissed, a very, very long kiss. I thought that would be it, that she had her wish and we'd part ways, but this was not to be, we spent the evening talking, dancing and kissing, we exchanged email addresses and at the end of the evening had one last kiss on the marina before she walked off into the night. I had no idea what I had done to be lucky enough to meet such a beautiful and fun lady, she was visually stunning and I would never have approached her in any other setting, she was way above my league, but on a cold winter's night in Stockholm, I was the person she wanted to be with. I turned around to join Darren and the Finnish girls but my vision was blocked by an image I'll never forget. As if the night could get no stranger, the universe had other ideas.

"Do you know who I am?" I'd heard this before, and it didn't end well then.

"I am Nostradamus, do you know my name-do you know me?"

"I've heard of you, but I can't say I know you pal" in fact, I didn't know him at all, I'd heard of the Nostradamus Prophecies, but I couldn't tell you what they were though, and I doubted that the man in front of me, a dishevelled, grey and nicotine stained bearded tramp with his vodka breath, was the real deal, I had serious doubts indeed.

"I am Nostradamus and I hold here the fate of the universe." He held up a plastic carrier bag half filled with the fate of the universe. "I hold the fate of the universe, and now I, Nostradamus, entrust it to you." And with this, he pushed the bag into my hand and also walked off into the night.

"What's in the bag?" Asked Darren when he'd stopped laughing.

"I'm not looking, I have to take good care of it, it's my duty." I'd seen Pulp Fiction several times and when John Travolta finally opens the briefcase and that gold light shone into his face, well that didn't happen to me that night, when I finally looked inside, I found the fate of the universe was an empty vodka bottle, an empty cigarette packet and half a shovels worth of grit. I nonchalantly tossed the lot into a rubbish bin. The fate of the universe was beyond reach.

After Stockholm we headed south to Copenhagen and set up in a shopping mall. Once we'd unloaded, again, Darren and I headed off in search of refreshment and found an Irish Pub. We ended up in a music venue a few doors away a night or two later, I made friends with some students from Hamburg before getting totally twatted and attempting to dance on a table to Sweet Home Alabama. I say attempted, because my foot slipped on the way up and I crashed face first onto the edge of the table, splitting open a big piece of my forehead. A concerned punter attempted to dress the wound and stop the bleeding, but my blood was 70% Jack Daniels by this point and there was no way it was going to congeal, no matter how long I stood still. After Copenhagen we headed back to Munich and unloaded, then were instructed to go to Strasbourg for a reload back to the UK, we were finally heading home after 28 days of being away. I'd had Green Day's American Idiot album on constant replay throughout this trip and can never hear *"Home, we're coming home again…"* without being transported back to the snow covered lands of Northern Europe, my last long trip on the road.

I had decided to quit my job at CES. I could work for Tara and Pat as an agency driver, they'd get a good service, earn a percentage and build a good reputation with their clients, I'd earn a good rate of pay plus with my CPC Qualifications, I could rent myself out as a freelance Transport Manager, everyone was a winner. I soon had a £400 a month income without having to get out of bed, plus whatever I earned driving. Life was good.

Heading over to the office one afternoon to pick up a check, I was minding my own business and just crossing a roundabout when another car flew past on the inside and cut me off, I slammed on my brakes so as to avoid hitting the blue BMW as it crossed my path and turned right ahead of me. The red mist descended and the chase was on. I followed the car onto a backstreet behind some shops. The car pulled in and I pulled up behind him. I got out and approached the other driver.

"What the fuck d'you think you're playing at, you fucking idiot?" *(Remember that diplomatic streak I'm renowned for? Me neither…)*   The Young guy in the car wound down his window and shrugged me off. "Why

don't you just mind your own business?" He said.   "You
made it my business when you tried to fucking kill me back there!" "Just fuck
off or I will fucking kill you!" He'd pulled a knife from the interior and
opened the car door. Realising the threat, I shoved the door and trapped his
leg, pulled my phone from my belt and dialled 999. He continued to make
threats against me but fought hard to get out the car. A Police car was sent
immediately and our conversation recorded as eventually I had to let the guy
out of the car, he was desperate to get somewhere and I wouldn't let him out
of my sight, each time he turned to wave his knife I stepped back, the
frustration in him becoming more apparent all the while. Finally, he rang a
buzzer on a side door next to one of the shops and darted inside. When the
police arrived I told them where he was and he was apprehended. His car was
searched and turned up some interesting results. It was believed he was a
Heroin courier and the police had been after him for a while. Thanks to my
intervention, he was going on holiday at one of her majesty's facilities. I had
no remorse, the guy was an idiot, if I had been him, I would not have been so
keen to draw so much attention to myself, some people just love to advertise
their own downfall in advance.
I headed off to the Isle Of Wight, to the UK Sailing Academy in Cowes. On
arrival, I was welcomed and given a quick rundown on the itinerary and met
the rest of the crew joining me aboard our home for the next week, a 67 ft
long Challenge Classic Yacht, called Whirlwind. The week absolutely flew by,
it was an incredible experience, sailing by day and night across the English
Channel. Our first day we headed out and around the Isle of Wight, taking in
a sail by The Needles before heading out into deep water. We crossed the
channel to Cherbourg where we docked overnight. The weather was kind to
us with wind speeds of no more than Force 6, just enough for us to earn our
sea legs and rid us of any surplus breakfast. I discovered a trait I'd never really
known about myself previously, that each first day at sea I would immediately
get an upset stomach and lean over the side rail, would feed the fish and then
be done with it. Once I discharged my excesses, I was right as rain and could
function perfectly well. It was as though I had to shed my landlubber skin
before my sea legs would fully function. From Cherbourg we headed back
across the channel and turned around along the south coast to head back over
to St Peter Port, Guernsey. The wind had picked up and at times hit a
maximum Force 9, we bounced and crashed over and through the waves, the
yacht ploughing on unnerved, it was a wonderful baptism to a possible career
on the briny. The last leg took us back to the South Coast and an overnight
stay at Brighton Marina. Paul, who I'd been friends with at Dafna, and came
to work aboard the Zorba 1, popped down to the marina to visit me. It was
great to see him and show him around the yacht. Compared to the schooner
we'd lived on previously, the Whirlwind seemed like a squat. The Zorba 1 was
much bigger and had a lot more room aboard for the number of crew. From

Brighton we took a leisurely sail back to Cowes and parted company with the rest of the crew. I loved that week at sea, the freedom and exhilaration of sailing at night, through wind and rain, big waves and calmer seas, I didn't want it to stop. Back at Cowes I noticed a sign on the wall at the Academy. Crew positions were being offered for the delivery of one of their 45 ft yachts to Antigua later that year. I put my name down immediately and was accepted. I was going to The Carribean, sailing across the Atlantic Ocean. Following in the footsteps of the many before me, Sir Walter Raleigh, Christopher Columbus, Blackbeard, Father Christmas *(OK, so he flies on a sled pulled by reindeer, but he still has to cross the ocean every year.)* It was a dream come true, an adventure beyond all my wildest imaginations.

Back in Coventry I knuckled down and started saving money to pay for my next adventure. I had to make sure I covered the bills for my time away, had enough to live on during the crossing, and pay for all the equipment I would need on the crossing as well as my part towards the cost, which itself was a fair amount- about £1000. I had 6 weeks to get everything in order.

Friday 15th October 2004, I collected my last cheque from the agency and paid it into the bank. Everything was in place, My bank account was not ideal, but it was comfortable enough to cover my costs, both at home and whilst away. I'd written my will, just in case, and deposited it with my solicitor. Saturday night I headed off to The Jailhouse for farewell drinks and entertainment. The Jailhouse was a live music pub in Coventry city centre, situated just behind the new magistrates' courts. The Jailhouse had become my home from home. There was a constant supply of live bands and great after show music, courtesy of the venue's promoter Paul Raggity, Meka's friend. Rich Mulligan would DJ and the sound man was a mate called Mick. Mick was the soundman for a famous Bhangra artist called Jazzy B. Mick toured the world with Jazzy B and whenever he played in the UK I would help with setting up the equipment. We went to a lot of Sikh weddings around the country, had a lot of fantastic Indian food and gallons of free Chivas Regal, courtesy of the Bride's family. One day I took Jordan to a festival in Slough, Jazzy B was performing to a crowd of 10's of thousands. When it was our turn to set up on stage, I gave Jordan the drummers' stool and told him where to put it, he walked bravely up on stage, set the stool down, turned to the audience and bowed. A huge cheer went up as my little man stole the show. "You know the agency's going bust, right?" H leaned in to inform me. He was serious, though a little wobbly as he clutched his JD & coke. His detox had only worked for a few short weeks, and now he was back on the booze, he would never kick the habit, and that was the tragedy of his life. The substance we both loved so dearly, would eventually take him down, it was just a matter of when. I double checked his comment.

"What do you mean it's going bust?"

"They're filing for bankruptcy on Monday morning." H belched in my ear.

I rang Tara immediately for confirmation. She told me nobody was meant to know, that's why she couldn't tell me, but yes, the agency was going down. There was nothing I could do. It wasn't my business but it had been my idea initially. I was off to the Carribean on Monday, that was not going to change, whether or not my pay cheque would be honoured at the bank. With the agency gone, I had to inform Tom in Poland that the work and dreams he'd built up, were also redundant. I could hear the disappointment in his voice and vowed to repay him for his efforts at a later date. This would mean flying out to Poland and handing over £1,000 worth of Zloty in return for a weekend of total drunkenness. *(Anyone with eyes keen enough the following Spring, to have spotted a very drunken Englishman rolling about in the background during the World Beachball Championships in Poland, may be witness to the promise having been fulfilled.)* The idea and dream that had been taken from me, was over. I was once again at square 1, with a clean slate to move forward.

9 Friggin' In The Riggin'

Nimrods Kiss

Life is the wind's warm kisses on skin

Touched by the heavens cooling, she brings

The freedom of thunder in the ears as she sings.

Silent, Invisible, only noticed within.

Beauty is vision-eyes brimming life

Bringing to vision the beauty of life.

The hills that surround us, the valleys that mourn

The rise of the sunlight, the peace that is dawn.

Chaos is living when living's not life

And beauty succumbs to the shadows of night.

By day feel the sunlight, by night feel the rain

The crisp morning dew and the wind once again.

Life is the wind she kisses blue skies,

Flirts with the Earth and strokes mountain sides.

Touching the skin and cooling the soul

She scatters and turns, but never grows old.

Age is the rockface, the changing of tides,

The bird on the wing-the height of it's rise.

Smell of the seasons and cities that die,

Carried on winds through blue mountain skies.

Stand on the rocks and sing me her praise,

Hold dear to this moment the rest of your days.

For life is the winds warm kisses on skin,

Touched by the heavens, now life can begin.

Monday 18th October, Coventry ,UK

Woke up early and drove to Portsmouth for the ferry to Isle Of Wight. Felt strange to be leaving again on such a long journey, not entirely convinced this is going to be a two-way ticket, the sea is a cruel mistress and I may have not been her most loyal muse. Once on the island I took the chain ferry across to Cowes, and drove the last short stretch to the Academy. I parked on the top of the car park, facing down so that I can roll down if the battery dies and jump start the engine on my own. Booked in at reception, claimed my bed for the night and retired to the bar. Sat on the balcony as the sun set, throwing long shadows across the boats in the marina. Tomorrow would be a big day, hard to sleep with the excitement, so much to look forward to.

Tuesday 19th October, Cowes I-O-W, UK

Met with the crew, Mike and Helen were a couple travelling on the first leg to Las Palmas only, Mike is an experienced sailor and will be 2nd Skipper on the opposite watch with Nigel, a long haired crewman from the Isle Of Man. Nigel has a great sense of humour- we get along really well. Robert is an older man, a retiree living in Germany, he's on my watch and seems affable enough. Our Skipper, Paul, is ex-Army, an instructor at the Academy and a very competent sailor. I daresay he could do this trip alone, single-handed, but then where's the fun in that for me? Our home for the next however long is Falcon, a 45ft Elan sailing yacht with 4 berths, a galley, heads and navigation desk. Paul took us through the basic introductions and layout of the boat, where the pumps were, the salt water and fresh water supply, shower, gas, food storage etc etc. Paul claimed the rear cabin by the engine room, the warmest place onboard, and least affected by the roll of the boat on the water. Helen and Mike took the other cabin in the stern, Myself and Nigel were to share the forward cabin on the starboard side *(that's the right one)* , and Robert was alone in the Port forward cabin *(that's the wrong one)*. If port and Starboard confuse you, think of it this way, Port is red and has fewer letters than Starboard, which is green. Which hand has the most letters, the left or right? Now you're on your way to being a real Deckhand. *(I did spell that right, didn't I?)* Waved off the maina by a handful of students and some of the Academy staff, felt kind of surreal, was this really it? I guess so. We sailed West and put in to Weymouth Harbour, the weather was deteriorating and we had to take shelter, the outlook for the next few days isn't great either.

Wednesday 20th October Weymouth, UK

_ Not much to report today, held captive in Weymouth by poor weather. Met office and coastguard reporting winds up to 70mph coming in on our nose if we make a move for Dartmouth, as Paul had planned. Air pressure has dropped to-and remaining around 996 Isobars, that means it's very low pressure and the atmosphere is rushing in to fill the hole, this is how wind is created without a bag of Kale and a catering sized tin of beans. We've discovered a leak on the Port heads *(nautical name for toilet/ bathroom/ shithouse)* which turned out to be a broken pump. Mike and Paul replace the pump with a spare from our spares locker. All other checks are OK but for a slight leak in #3 diesel injector on the engine. Retired to the Pub for a crew briefing. Mike and Helen quit not-smoking and are both back on the fags. Robert reported as being heard snoring in the pub's toilet, that'll be the wine what did it! Paid a visit to the local bank today, transferred £1000 to my account….. *(where from, and can I do it again, now , please?)*
New Nautical terminology picked up from Paul today;
SOOT - Shit Out Of Tins.
YMCA-Yesterday's Meals Cooked Again.
WAFU- Wet And Fucking Useless.
WAFI- Wind Assisted Fucking Idiot.
Whoopi Goldberg- Black Coffee No Sugar.

Thursday 21st October, Weymouth, UK

Still in Weymouth, gale force winds came through overnight gusting windforce 8-9. *(Very fucking windy)* Coastguard reporting Storm Force 10 at Dover and no, that's not a fucking boyband. More of the same expected tomorrow by the looks of it. Kept ourselves busy today by learning Buoyage and then took a bus ride to Portland Bill to look out over the channel. Any doubts about not continuing along the coast were firmly put to rest, it was bloody grim out there on the water. The wind and waves were horrendous. Took photos of the breaking waves before having a cream tea and returning to Falcon. Barometer reading 1002 at 0800hrs, 1005 at 1800hrs. It seems such a shame to be laid up so soon but that's the way it goes, respect the sea or continue at your peril. There's no room for error or stupidity, safety first. Robert and I retire to the pub for a night cap, c'est la vie.

Friday 22nd October, Weymouth, UK

Wind eased a little overnight, still not a good forecast but it's looking promising for tomorrow. Took apart and cleaned 2 of the 4 winches in the cockpit area before rain stopped play. Decided to all eat out tonight as it's Paul's birthday tomorrow and it looks like we could be leaving on the mornings' high tide. Barometer reading 1005 at 1700hrs, fairly constant all day. Another yacht moored alongside at 1700hrs, they'd arrived from Torquay and reported winds of 45-50 Knots all day.*(A knot being a Nautical mile , or 1.852Km/ph)* We are all hoping to get our window in the weather tomorrow so we can get going again, we're enjoying ourselves but would much rather be sailing, it's what we came here for. Mike and Helen have quit smoking again.

Saturday 23rd October, Weymouth,UK Still

A cold front arrived at 1207 *(I put a warm jersey on her and sent her home- ba-boom-tish! I'm here all week folks…)* Barometer reading 1003.4, unfortunately this made no change to our predicament. Met office chart showed at least 5 areas of low pressure reaching from Biscay to Norway and across to the Balkans. A high pressure area over the Great Lakes, and another over the Black Sea are squeezing all the heavy wind and rain over the route we need to take. This really is getting dull now, it's like we're doomed already. We'd hoped and expected to be away on tonight's tide at the latest, but now it could be Monday or Tuesday yet still. Mike and Paul are making the most and teaching us Navigation and Seamanship skills, so we are learning a little each day. We bought a card for Paul's birthday to cheer him up a little, it must be hard, so close to home but so far away from his wife and kids. Mike and Helen are smoking again.

Sunday 24th October, Weymouth, UK, again still

Moved across the marina to fill our water tanks today. The marina is calm but it's definitely blowing a gale out in the channel. Several weekend yachties trotted out this morning, all smiles and no life-jackets, only to return later looking absolutely battered and wearing their safety gear. We stripped and cleaned the remaining winches, replacing 3 springs we found that were faulty. Paul gave a deck briefing, some instruction on primary and secondary ports *(nothing to do with the bottled variety, I'm afraid, more nautical jargon)* managed to miss the shipping forecast at 1700hrs as Nigel's radio played up and his batteries died. Spent the evening practising secondary port calculations, it's all rock'n'roll in this cockpit honey. Expecting to be away 0800hrs Tomorrow.

Monday 25th October, fucking Weymouth, UK

Another bad start to the day, Met office reports and local conditions too poor but we have a real chance of getting out on tonights tide instead. There are warnings of a gale approaching which may lay us up in Falmouth for a day or two, oh joy of joys, will we never leave this cursed Isle? Slipped our berth at 2000hrs and celebrated with some gummy bears. Conditions dead calm, almost eerie as we motored out past the Condor Ferries Catamaran and the evening fishermen on the pier. The water and wind picked up by Portland and once we were into open sea we hit several slammers, big waves that stop you in your tracks. Robert, Paul and I took first watch. I took the helm at 2100-0000hrs when we changed watch. I love steering the boat, regardless of the conditions, it's the best job onboard. 0030hrs Robert threw up in the heads, one too many gummy bears can do that to a man. I waited until we changed watch at 0300hrs and threw up *(fed the fish)* over the side of the boat. Mike and Helen quit smoking again.

Tuesday 26th October, at sea

Out in the channel and we are all feeling much better, except the gummy bears, they're all dead, shit happens. Finally doing what we came for, sailing the open sea, even if we are hugging the coast, we are out on the wet stuff. Passed 3 Naval vessels on the approach to Eddystone Lighthouse, they were on exercises along with a Merlin Helicopter which seemed to be running errands between them, probably bootlegging Pusser's Rum or some seriously good contraband confiscated offshore somewhere. We heard some shells being fired somewhere but not on our watch. Back on watch at 0600-0900hrs. Had lunch at 1200hrs and finally found my sea legs. Not bothered so much by the motion or the noise of the engine, not even the slammers, everything is going well. ETA Falmouth 15-1600hrs, motor sailing all the way, looks like I got the best turn on the helm last night, life is good. Arrived Falmouth 1600hrs on the marina. Refuelled with diesel, hosed down and secured the decks. Just a matter of waiting for our next window to start the next run, actually feeling as if we are on our journey now, I hope we can get moving again soon, nobody came here to sit in the harbour, we are all keen to get some miles between us and Blighty, all looking forward to some warm water sailing. Mike and Helen celebrate with a cigarette each.

Wednesday 27th October, Falmouth, UK

Here we are again, captives of poor weather, sheltering in the confines of Falmouth harbour. The wind is howling, rain drizzling into every tiny gap available to it. Another 24 hours lost. Barometer reading 98.3 at 1150hrs. Paul collected synoptics from the marina office. Forecast shows a low of 956 sitting right over where we want to go until Friday night or Saturday, with highs all around it has nowhere to go, no chance but to sit where it is and slowly fill. We are stuck again. Thankfully we seem well protected here on our berth. Some other boats haven't fared so well, a couple have broken free and come to rest on the beach and rocks about the river's edge. Yacht Souza reported a gust of wind of 55knots. Barometer reading at 1300hrs 981, 1845hrs 976 and dropping all the time. As bad as the weather is, Paul believes the worst is yet to come.

Thursday 28th October, Falmouth, UK

The day began at 0330hrs to watch the lunar eclipse. The wind had shifted around to the west (270 degrees). The eclipse itself was something of a letdown, a small moon only slightly shaded and intermittent cloud cover spoiling the view. Helen, Nigel and myself returned to our cabins at 0410hrs. Woke again at 1015hrs, had breakfast, did engine checks, cleaned the boat. Took a shower ashore *(no, I did not carry the cubicle down the high street)* and returned for lunch. Barometer read 981 at 1230hrs, wind still howling, strong gusts. Russian skipper Fedor Konyukhov, has given up and gone home for a month, he's coming back to attempt to break the Round The World Single Handed Record. His yacht is moored next to ours and it's huge, a real monster. Personally I wouldn't like to sail it but there are many people that would. Barometer reading 977 at 2000hrs. Raining on and off, windy and quite cold too, a miserable day really. I have found out that my rubber sailing boots are great at keeping out the rain, but absolutely useless at keeping my feet warm. I'm wearing thick wooly socks, Thermals and my sailing gear but still my feet are freezing. Should have bought something with a fur lining, it's hard to stay positive when you have to sit still with cold feet for 4 hours at a time.

Friday 29th October, Falmouth, UK, again

Started the day with some general tidying up and cleaning. Victualling run *(shopping to you lot)* followed by a trip to the laundry. Paul decides we can make it out tonight on the 2030hrs tide, weather calm, dry mostly. We prepare the boat for departure, briefing at 1600hrs. Slipped our berth at 2000hrs after a good stuffing of Fish & Chips in Falmouth. Barometer reading 989 and rising through the night. Wind ESE (East-southeast) 18knots, moderate sea, fed the fishes at 0400hrs, port side rail, quelle surprise.

Saturday 30th October, English Channel

Jordan's birthday today, the first time I haven't been with him on his birthday, it plays on my mind as I look around at the sea and sky. The wind has eased a little, during early morning Paul set a Preventer on the Boom to stop accidental Gybing, where the wind is light and the sail swings violenting from one side of the boat to the other, this can cause injury or death to the crew, as well as sapsize the vessel. We are rolling around like a cork in a swimming pool, but at least the sky is blue and we are finally sailing again. Lost our Spinnaker pole over the side this afternoon. I was on the helm and Paul decided to inspect the mast and rigging. He pulled on a line to check it was tight but the pole had not been secured, pulling the line released it and it bounced over the side of the boat. I turned about to try to retrieve it, like an impromptu Man Overboard exercise, but it has already been swallowed up by Davy Jones' Locker. Paul wasn't his usual self after this, if he could he would have kicked a cat, it was that bad. He now had to call the Academy and request a replacement be shipped out ASAP. Later on we sailed over the Continental shelf, our depth gauge went from 140m to 4000+ We now had 4Km of water beneath us, an awesome feeling indeed. Barometer reading 1013 and the air temperature has risen too. We are all feeling good now, living the dream. Saw our first shooting star on the midnight to 0400hrs watch. We even had a Dolphin swimming alongside until we set the engine at 0340hrs. Clocked up 194 sea miles Midnight to midnight.

Sunday 31st October, English Channel

Slow to start myself this morning but soon got into the swing of things. Took the helm around 1000hrs and within minutes caught sight of a Minke Whale, the first I'd ever seen. It broke water to blow it's air about 25ft to our Port bow, resubmerged and passed beneath the boat. It was fantastic to see, about 30ft long, grey/white in colour, sliding back under the surface. This brief encounter made everything we'd been through worthwhile. We made 140 Nautical miles, 314 Nm total, we are making excellent time now and should be in Cascais Wednesday. Barometer reading 1013 at 0800hrs, 1019 at 1300hrs. Lots of Dolphins around us today. Received a radio call from a Tanker, another Yacht has been lost at sea somewhere nearby, they'd issued a Pan-Pan radio call but were lost in the Bay of Biscay, nearby. *(A Pan Pan is a radio broadcast sent out by a vessel to alert others that the vessel is in difficulty, it is not used when life is in imminent danger, in that case a vessel would use a Mayday Distress Call.)* There's nothing we can do except keep our eyes open, the other yacht is 2 days late already and there's little hope of finding them out here. It was a sobering reminder of the dangers about us, and the reason we'd sheltered as long as we had in Falmouth. During bad weather, it can be safer to ride the storm in deep water, rather than heading for shelter in shallow water, waves nearer the shore become larger, faster and more dangerous as the sea bed rises. The missing vessel was a yacht on a delivery voyage, the skipper paid by the mile to deliver the vessel to it's next port, usually in time for it's owner or the next crew to join the vessel for it's next intended journey/charter.On this occasion 3 young sailors lost their lives trying to get to shore.

Monday 1st November, Approaching Finisterre

Pinch Punch 1st of the month and the miles are flying by, we are making good speed and should be in Cascais Wednesday PM. 1019-1020 on the barometer today, perfect blue sky sailing. Paul called in today and reported the loss of the Spinnaker Pole, a replacement is being sent to Las Palmas and should be there when we arrive. Rounded Finisterre this evening having taken a photo of a Gas Ship earlier in the day, oddly enough, one of their crew was taking a photo of us at the same time. No sign or word of the missing Yacht, no whales or Dolphins either, just lots of sunshine and merchant shipping.

Tuesday 2nd November, Bay of Biscay

1st watch 0000hrs to 0400hrs. Alone at the helm as we passed Cape Finisterre, a school of Dolphins all about me, I could not have been happier if I tried, there are certain moments in life when you just wish you could relive and share that feeling, that moment, when everything is better than you could ever have dreamed. Feeling the ocean beneath me, riding the waves, the wind in my face and Dolphins all about me, swimming on their sides looking up at me looking down at them. The temptation to jump overboard and join them flickered in my mind briefly, but I knew, this is their world, I am a visitor, it was not my place to step beyond their entrance, no matter how inviting they seemed. The Barometer dropped 1Mb at 0300hrs, it now read 1014. There was a brilliant circle of high altitude light and cloud refracting from the moon. It was a warning, bad weather was once again heading our way. The window to cross the Bay of Biscay was now closed, we headed for shelter to Bayona Beach altering course at 0800hrs, the weather worsening all the while. By 1200hrs we were tacking into the wind and waves, white water rafting on a 45ft yacht, it was exhilarating, the most adrenaline filled time of the entire trip thus far, racing up and down the waves with only the power of the wind driving us along. We tried to head for Vialla De Costillo but were beaten back by the weather, we turned around and berthed at Bayona at 1800hrs. There was doubt about it, just when I think this trip has peaked, it gets better and better. Weymouth-Falmouth-Bayona 916 Nm, 94 hours at Sea.

Wednesday 3rd November, Bayona, Spain

We slipped our berth at 1300hrs after refuelling with 60 litres of diesel from our Jerrycans. 115 litres of freshwater used, less than 20L per person (4L per day, each). We were escorted out of the Spanish shelter by a pair of Porpoises putting on a show of synchronised swimming and aerobics. Nearer the shore a huge flock of Gannets were dive bombing a shoal of fish. Very little wind to speak of, sea state moderate, lots of black clouds ahead, may get quite stormy later.

Thursday 4th November, Cascais, Portugal

Began the day on the 0000-0400hrs watch. The rain arrived in time to soak us to the core, cold, wet, thoroughly miserable and glad to see the end of this watch. Sleep was instantaneous and deep. Up again at 0800hrs for breakfast and saw that the clouds were now behind us, the air was warming up more and more as the day progressed. A group of about 15-20 Porpoises joined us but vanished as soon as I got my camera. Managed to take photos of Berlenga and Farilhao, archipelagos off the coast of Peniche, and Cabo Cavaliero, Portugal. As we passed between the Islands and the mainland we heard a diesel engine thundering past beneath us, a submarine. There were no airplanes or other ships within sight. We passed Cabo Cavaliero at 1533hrs, barometer reading was 1018/9 all day, hardly any wind at all. Paul made a curry for supper, just as we sat down to eat we sailed through the middle of a different feeding frenzy. Hundreds of Gannets dive bombing relentlessly all about us, the ocean was awash with Tuna, Porpoises and other animals, it was an incredible sight to observe, the true life of the ocean within our very own reach. Amazing to witness and all too quickly over again, the tranquility of the waves kissing the sky returned as if nothing had even happened. We arrived in Cascais Marina at 2100hrs, in the pub by 2120hrs. Bayona- Cascais 259Nm, 14 night hours, 18 daytime hours.

Friday 5th November, Cascais, Portugal

Discovered our compressor bracket had sheared from the engine. Paul took it to get welded back together. UKSA advised us to have a new one made in Antigua when we get there. Cleaned the boat and Prepared to slip tonight. Barometer reading 1015 at 1550hrs. 750 miles to Las Palmas, are you ready for it? Hell yeah! Unfortunately though, the boat isn't. Our mechanic friend will not have a replacement plate ready until tomorrow lunchtime, ergo, we are here overnight. I can sense a few words of complaint, from my liver. It's a dry boat, no booze on board at any time, but ashore we may partake, so long as we are sober on watch. Nigel and I head to the Bar Do Lata, shortly followed by the rest of the crew. We get back to our bunks just before sunrise having all climbed over a gate beside the Castle rather than walking around the block. There's a 30ft off the side and we were all pissed, which probably helped. Oh, and I lost the funnel for our diesel tank whilst refuelling today, I dropped it over the stern. Oops!

Saturday 6th November, Cascais, Portugal

Awake grudgingly, with a sore head. Still waiting for the mechanic. Nigel bought a new funnel in Cascais and we succeeded in topping up the diesel before going for a McDonalds in Cascais. Still no sign of the bracket when we return. Tensions are mounting at the loss of time, Helen and Mike need to be getting back to the UK soon and are getting a bit edgy. After a few drinks and a meal in a Mexican restaurant, they relax a little.Robert manages to leave his bag behind in the restaurant, by the time he realises it's already closed and he will have to return in the morning. Nigel and I end up in the pub again. I take a walk alone into Cascais during the night, sit on the beach for a while and admire my surroundings. I am so lucky to be here. I get back and am in bed at 0630hrs.

Sunday 7th November, still in bloody Cascais-but at least it ain't Weymouth

Up again at 1000hrs to help Nigel set up the RIB, Rigid Inflatable Boat. He needs Paul to sign him off in the RIB and then he qualifies as Competent Crew. We row around the marina and find the Funnel we lost Friday night. Robert returns from the restaurant with his bag intact, everything's coming together. Mike and Helen rename Nigel and myself The Blues Brothers. After lunch, we deflate and stow the RIB in the forward sail locker and then Paul briefs us after supper. Tomorrow we will get the bracket repaired and fitted, then we are off. He's not a happy bunny at the minute, we seem to have had too many hold-ups for his liking. Paul is definitely a do-er, not a waiter. He regales us of the time he was in the Caribbean and sailed through a hurricane. His crew below decks while he stayed at the wheel, being washed by waves and battered by 100mph winds, he held his post, held that wheel and rode that demon for 36 hours straight. You cannot help but respect a man like that, a real fighter, not some prick who bullies people with his fists, but someone who faces the storm head on and does not quit. Early to bed tonight, 2130hrs.

Monday 8th November and still not gone

Nigel and I do the victualling in Cascais care of the Coffee shop and Post Office. Paul collected the bracket from the workshop only to find out it had been ready since 1600hrs on Saturday, but nobody had informed us. Paul, Mike and myself put it back together again before a late lunch and finally we slip our berth at 1430, stopping at the refuelling island before heading out to the open ocean. Once we get a mile or so off the coast, the Dolphins return. We ran on the engine for a while, heading 210 degrees for the next 4 days straight. Engine off at 1930hrs. Discover the stern shower has been pumping water and the stern water tank is now empty. Bloody good job we realised now and not after leaving Las Palmas, we would not have had enough water to cross the ocean and would have had to ration every drop. Paul decided to disconnect the power supply to the shower in Las Palmas, we can't risk it happening again.

Tuesday 9th November, Atlantic Ocean

Saw 7 shooting stars on our watch last night, no other vessels anywhere to be seen today. Had some stowaways aboard today, Paul splattered 4 flies in the Galley today and Robert and I were attacked by a Flying Fish, all that's missing is the Locusts and a few sacrificial virgins to ensure that the sky doesn't fall on our heads, and the sun will rise again in the morning. This is most definitely the life, blue skies, blue seas, large swells and a good crew. Barometer reading is steady around 1014/5 just about in line with the Straits Of Gibraltar, passing over the Gorringe Ridge where underwater volcanic activity has lifted the sea bed from around 4000m to only 26m, plenty enough room for us to get through, but it can have an effect on the water as it passes over. By 1600hrs we are 200 miles out, only 550 more to Las Palmas. Caught sight of a ship on the starboard horizon, about 20 miles off our Beam at 1640hrs. *(The beam is the middle of the length of a vessel.)* Exciting stuff indeed! Back onto late watch and it's like Piccadilly Circus out there, 3 ships on the horizon, we'll have to be very careful so as not to hit any of them in all this ocean.

<u>Wednesday 10th November, Atlantic Ocean.</u>

Saw only 5 shooting stars last night, the sky was cloudy and no visible moon either, which meant we were sailing blind. I would describe this as the equivalent of drawing a line on a road map, say from London to Manchester for example. That is the route *(our Heading)* but we cannot see the sky to take readings from the celestial bodies, that's like painting your windscreen black and attempting to drive the route with only the contours of the land to gauge your position on the road. Yes we have Satellite Positioning, GPS, but that is like using a SatNav system, you're putting your faith in a device that may not be accurate or reliable at any given moment. Didn't sleep too well, no wind in the headsail, too much noise and distraction on deck. Barometer reading is up to 1018/9. We are surfing a lot of waves but the wind isn't very good, gusty and calm, heading 230 degrees but veering 240 to keep the wind in our sails at times. It was our turn to put a reef in last night *(reducing the amount of sail available to the wind)* usually the other watch have been doing this, the times they are a-changing. Nearly collided with an oil tanker today, a whole ocean about us and he chooses to cut across my bows. We saw the ship on the radar but couldn't physically see her because of the swell of the waves, by the time we did it was almost too late, I turned the helm to Port and we ran almost alongside her, close enough to read their breakfast menu. The wake of the ship threw us around quite a bit, it was better than a fun ride at the Fair. She was registered in Singapore, the Sala, about half a mile long and 50m wide, that was a close call. The swell is getting bigger, winds improving. 194Nm today, we are steaming away here, final mileage midnight to midnight 203Nm. I can't express just how much fun this is, I don't know I have ever lived before now, nothing seems to compare to the feelings I am experiencing.

<u>Thursday 11th November, Atlantic Ocean</u>

Bump and grind! Nigel managed to get thrown off the wheel by a squall, the boat spun 360 degrees on the spot. Unable to get it back into the wind, Mike used the engine to power the boat round. Below deck, our watch were all thrown out of our bunks oblivious to everything but the noise and rude awakening. The wind is up, no moon again so more blindfold sailing in 30 knot winds, fantastically exhilarating stuff, waves around the 20ft mark, superb sailing and surf. Came within a mile and a half of another tanker this evening then I got hit by a rogue wave I hadn't seen until it was too late. It hit us on the port quarter and even Paul thought we were going over. I managed to pull the boat back around with only a few words of complaint from the Galley, I guess that was payback for Nigel turfing us out of bed. For my penance, Paul took the helm and decided to gybe, I was sent forward on the deck to fit a preventer line to the headsail. Despite getting washed by a few waves, I made it back to the cockpit in one piece. We were back on the foredeck again later, myself, Robert and Nigel. The furling headsail line jammed in it's block and it took all our strength to release it. Paul set preventers on the shroud covers to stop them lifting with the headsail sheets. A busy day all things considered, but this is no holiday and I've got the bruises to prove it. Finished the day with 2 hours of blinding helmsmanship. Unfortunately, Paul lost his favourite mug to the fishes and the port canvas dodger almost got washed away by a rogue wave hitting the starboard quarter. Had an amazing experience just before the end of our watch too. Was it a UFO, was it a shooting star? An extremely bright light lit up the boat, it was like a fluorescent green flare/light had illuminated the cockpit for about 10 seconds. Paul then noticed a flash on our starboard beam which repeated 5 minutes later. We checked the radar, nothing else anywhere near us. Maybe we'd been zapped by aliens, would we arrive in Las Palmas 10 years late with no memory of where we'd been, had we been probed? Anyone for Bagels?...... 21Nm Midnight to Midnight. Robert clocked a top speed of 12.8knots. Barometer down to 1013. Mike later reported having had a Goldfinch resting on deck throughout his watch. Incredible, what an amazing time.

Friday 12th November, somewhere in the galaxy

Sailing with 3 reefs in the mainsail now. The wind and ocean displaying awesome power, where had the blue sky and sea gone? This wasn't in the brochure. Nigel repaired the Dodger only for me to wash away all his good work overnight. Hit by 2 more rogue waves and took on a ton of water along the port side, Paul took the full force of a wave and now thinks I have it in for him, there goes my CV! Maybe I should consider flipping burgers for a living. Robert managed to repeat my faux pas and Paul now seems to be wondering what he'd done so wrong in a previous lifetime to deserve us. Running alongside Lanzarote now, our ETA at Las Palmas is moving further back. Last night we were blasting along at 10-12 knots, gusts up to 53 knots, today we're plodding along at 7-8 knots with winds of no more than 20-25 knots. Looks like we'll be arriving in Las Palmas for breakfast instead of evening dinner. Barometer up to 1017, made it alongside Las Palmas at 0530 hrs.

Saturday 13th November, Las Palmas, Gran Canaria.

912Nm from Cascais, welcome to Las Palmas. Spent today victualling and topping up with fresh water etc. Moved off our berth by ARC organisers so we refuelled and anchored outside the marina. *(ARC is the Annual Rally for Cruisers. An annual race to cross the Atlantic which would be departing Las Palmas about the same time as we were, we were guaranteed a lot of company on the next leg.)* I took a taxi to the airport to meet Martin, our replacement 2nd Skipper as Mike and Helen were packing to return home to the UK. Martin Noyle is an accomplished yachtsman and also managed the Ellen MacArthur Foundation's website. (Dame) Ellen MacArthur reached global recognition after becoming the fastest sailor to circumnavigate the globe single handedly, she was also a patron of the UKSA, alongside Princess Margaret. As Martin and I return, Mike and Helen take the same taxi back to the airport. It's a shame to see them go but it was great to meet them, we commiserate with a cigarette. Nigel and I rebuilt the RIB and fit the outboard motor before retiring for supper and a few well earned beers as we got to know our new crew member. Tomorrow we will be joined by Christian, he was due in from Germany and would be taking Helen's place on board, but not her berth, instead he would be sharing with Robert who'd been on his own up until now. Back to the boat with a wet arse thanks to Martin's RIB handling skills.

Sunday 14th November, Las Palmas, Gran Canaria

24 degrees celsius and rising, the sun is out and it's hot, hot, hot! ARC people are everywhere. We all go to the laundry, Nigel and I head off for a wander around the backstreets of Las Palmas. We decide on a liquid lunch and discuss the possibility of writing a book about mis-translated street signs and menus. We chuckle at the idea of going into a restaurant and ordering the equivalent of a Lamb roast with all the trimmings and custard instead of gravy. Pouring mint sauce or Horseradish on a strawberry cheesecake. I mean, how often have you gone into a restaurant somewhere and gambled on your order, hoping it wasn't Cheese on toast with a rich brandy sauce, cod and figs? The possibilities are endless. Paul collected Christian from the airport, Nigel and I went to meet them at the marina and were reprimanded by someone up a mast for speeding, naughty Nigel. Went for an evening meal in Las Palmas, it turns out Christian's father is a famous filmmaker in Germany, can't say any of us had heard of him, but Christian himself seemed like a nice enough guy. Martin fell off the jetty into the marina attempting to secure a drifting RIB that had become untethered. Returned to Falcon to write postcards for everyone back home. Tomorrow we will go shopping and prep for our next crossing.

Monday 15th November, Las Palmas, Gran Canaria

Once bitten twice shy, so they say. Today began with a trip to the laundry and then to the fruit market and post office. I ferried Nigel and Robert back to the boat, without getting shouted at for speeding. We exchanged our gas bottles and returned to prep the engine. Began washing and stowing the fruit and veg before finding out we couldn't go anywhere until Thursday as that was when the spinnaker pole would actually be arriving. It was due to be shipped out and would therefore not arrive until the 24th, so Paul demanded it be air freighted to us and we would leave Thursday with or without it. Sun , sea and sangria, we were prisoners in this hellhole, how would we possibly cope?

117

Tuesday 16th November, Las Hangover Canaria

Woke up with a headache, self inflicted as usual. Ferry everyone ashore in the RIB, only myself and Nigel remain onboard. We are called over to another yacht, the skipper is an Ex-UKSA student doing a delivery from Croatia to Tortola. He tells us the job prospects of students rely entirely on their own ability to find work. Mileage is of the most importance, so I may have to rethink my own expectations here. If I take a gamble on working as a professional skipper, I need to build up my connections. Took a walk along the beach over to the other side of town, snapping some photos of the beach, the mountains and a club called 'Dancing Fanys'. Nobody will believe me if I don't produce any evidence. Back to Falcon for a swim off the stern before sundowners ashore. Supper aboard the boat followed by a blast of my Burdock CD and a glass of rum on deck. Perfect.

Wednesday 17th November, you know where we are

Maintenance and more prepping for our trans-ocean voyage. Oiled the cockpit table and step, tightened every loose screw and nut on deck, including Nigel. Did engine checks and galley cleaning. Paul contacted the customs agent only to find our TNT Tracking number is wrong and so we have absolutely no idea where our spinnaker pole is now. Also, the outboard engine on the RIB is a 2 stroke and has somehow managed our abuse without having a single drop of oil in it. Nigel has taken it to the garage to get some oil. At lunchtime we discover the Spinnaker pole is now at Stansted Airport, having arrived there at 2000hrs last night. Martin, the Customs agent is back on the case at 1600hrs after his siesta. A french yacht arrived to anchor next to us in the bay. The skipper ordered his young crewmate to drop anchor, she pressed all the right buttons but their anchor was still secured to the bow, on their second attempt the anchor drops into the water but fails to get a good grip. 3rd attempt and they succeed to get a secure hold but have lost their dinghy in the process. I dived overboard and retrieved the dinghy before it drifted out into the ocean. As a way of saying "Merci Beaucoup!" I am invited for drinks at 2200hrs. Christian is kept waiting on the jetty for our RIB to collect him, so I swam over to him to let him know that Nigel had gone to the garage with it. He'd been waiting 90 minutes and wandered off again once I spoke with him. Swam back to Falcon, knackered. Christian rigged a temporary kill chord on the RIB once it came back from the garage. I collected Nigel and Robert from the Marina later on to find Robert could hardly walk. On top of this he'd bought a gun from El Corte Ingles and proudly exhibited the bloody thing to the crew. I don't envy Paul right now, he's been put in a tricky spot. Robert should be sent home at this point, the carrying of arms on board a vessel at sea is a serious offence, especially if the weapon is not licenced and declared to customs. Paul wants to sleep on the matter and make a decision in the morning. Personally, I fear Robert is becoming a little unhinged and maybe a long sea voyage may not be the best thing for him right now. I retire to the French boat and have a pleasant evening drinking with my new friends before swimming home again in time for bed.

Thursday 18th November, OK Corral or is it the Alamo?

Still no spinnaker pole. At 1700hrs it is confirmed as arriving tomorrow on a commercial flight from Madrid at either 0600 or 1030hrs. The first flight would give us time to clear customs and leave tomorrow. The later flight would miss customs and mean we sail without it or have to wait until Monday or Tuesday to clear customs. Had a shower and shave before going shopping with Paul and Martin. By the time we return, Robert is a reformed character after last nights' episode. The Pistol went for a swim with the fishes. Tomorrow is D-Day *(again, talk about Groundhog Day, Bill Murray is an amateur compared to us lot!)* Prawn curry supper followed by an early night. Something strangely satisfying about pulling the heads off 200 sea creatures and then throwing them overboard for the fishes to eat, it feels like we are sharing our supper with the ocean. Night-night!

Friday 19th November Groundhog Day

Start the day with eager anticipation, cleaning, clearing, stowing, resting etc. Apparently there's snow back home in Cheltenham and Isle Of Man, ha-ha! I put on my warm shorts in a show of unity for my poor fellows back home in

Blighty. Wind is up to 19 knots on average. Lots of movement in the harbour. We practice hoisting the mainsail but it powers up and we drag the anchor a little so we have to take up about 5m of chain to avoid colliding with other boats around us. Paul returns from the agent 1145hrs, not a happy bunny, still no Spinnaker pole. 1500hrs we up anchor and motor to the fuel island to fill up with diesel and freshwater. I hang over the bow trying to lift the anchor, Martin is working the electrics and a disaster is looming at any moment. We ship the anchor and I count all my fingers, yep 12, all is good. We come alongside a pontoon and head out for sundowners as we wait for the elusive agent, Martin and the much needed spinnaker pole to arrive. Paul gets a call, the pole is arriving at 1915hrs from Madrid (?) but will be with us at 2015hrs. Sure enough, Martin arrives at 1900hrs with our boats registration doc's and Paul's passport. The truck arrives an hour later and the long awaited pole is gladly received and secured on deck. We are free to leave in the morning. Paul and I take a taxi ride out into the mountains to a pizzeria that makes the best Pizza in the whole of Espana. £20 for the taxi, £4 for the Pizza and dos cervesa por favor. Tony, the taxi driver plays Celine Dion- My Heart Will Go On, on the cassette player and then puts on a concerned but helpful voice as he asks if we want some nice young women before we leave on our bon voyage across the ocean. A class act, but even so, as clean as his young ladies may be, no thanks mate!

Saturday 20th November, D-fucking-Day at last!

 Wake up early and begin to clear up. Dismantle the RIB and stow it in the sail locker, everything else readied and stowed. Over to the diesel pontoon for 2'5 litres of water, every drop counts now. Before I get a chance to finish making a cuppa, we are away and out of Las Palmas and heading south again. We pass between Gran Canaria and Tenerife but the wind is very slight and after a short period with the new pole extended on the headsail to enable us to Goosewing *(sailing with the headsail to port and the mainsail to starboard or vice versa)* , we run the engine for a few hours. We catch sight of a pair of flying fish off our port bow. The sun is roasting hot but we are back on form, praise be to Jack Daniels, hallelujah brother! There was a beautiful sunset this evening, silvery blue sea, flat, calm and almost mirror like against a pink/red and orange horizon. There is no wind, only 4-5 knots, a totally calm ocean all around. Something black popped it's head out of the water about 20m behind us, then submerged, it was probably a seal. Bed at 2000hrs, back on watch at

0000hrs. Our position at midnight 27 deg 44.1minutes North, 16 deg 41.9 minutes West.

Sunday 21st November, Atlantic Ocean

 Absolutely incredible light show tonight. Heading to a little Island called Hierro, last dry land now before the Carribean. We need to refuel due to the lack of wind. Caught sight of lights from the island at 0230hrs. The moon set beyond the horizon and a couple of minutes later an incredible shooting star fell on our port side, green and as bright as a firework streaking across the sky. This was followed by an orange one further south and almost immediately a 3rd, ordinary white shooting star streaking across the sky overhead. It was beautiful. We also had the return of Bioluminescence, with the light from the moon gone tiny diamonds of natural light sparkled in the churned up waters of our wake. We'd seen this before, many times, and on a moonless night on a quiet ocean, it was good to see again. We run into the harbour at La Restinga, the island towering 1200m above us. We moor alongside to find nothing is open. No diesel, no water, nothing until tomorrow. Nigel, Christian and myself head off up the road out of town to the top of a volcano. The view was incredible. Volcanic rock floes running down to the sea, liquid set into solid rock, black, yellow, red, green and all tones between. I cannot believe how incredibly beautiful this place is, and still untouched by the onslaught of tourism that decimates the other islands to the north. Rob joined us at the top of the volcano having taken a different route to us, he looked around, acknowledging the beautiful scenery before descending again alone, down a different path to our own. We found a small bar in the town and enjoyed a couple of beers before heading back to Falcon. Filled 50 litres of diesel from our jerrycans into the tank but lost the bottom of the funnel over the stern. It seems that Nigel and I are doomed to failure when it comes to refilling the diesel tank. Took a shower under the tap on the marina before going to town for supper. All in all a fantastic day. Our position tonight 184Nm travelled. 27 deg 36.9 min North, 17 deg 45.8 min West.

Monday 22nd November, La Restinga, El Hierro

Awoke at 0150 and 0510hrs by the sound of the anchor running along the harbour wall. One each of the bow and stern lines had chaffed through, so we reset them, taking in the slack before going back to bed. Up again at 0800hrs to refill the water tanks from our emergency supply, approx 45 litres used. Topped up the diesel cans (50L) and slipped La Restinga 1030hrs, out into the big wide ocean for the final time. Head and Mainsail goosewinged with the pole out. Sunscreen applied, we assume the position and tan ourselves in the midday sun. Bad news came over the VHF radio, some ARC crews were reporting an area of low pressure coming in which would affect all areas down to 20 deg North which would put the wind directly in our face along with a threat of rain. This is not a good position to be in. As you may know, a sailing yacht needs the wind to come from either side or the stern. For a yacht to travel with the wind head on, it needs to Tack sideways across the direction of the wind in order to move forward. Hopefully we can pick up the trade winds before it's too late and get across the pond before christmas. Took my first sunsight with the sextant today. It felt really good to actually see how it works. *(To use a sextant to take a sunsight, you have to calculate the height of the sun at any particular time. The sextant can be set to measure the distance from the bottom of the sun's circumference to the horizon. Once that measurement is taken, you record the exact time and refer to the ship's Celestial Navigation Logs. By comparing the declination to the exact time, the log will give you your exact position anywhere on the surface of the Earth.)* Our position at Midnight 26 deg 50 min North 19 deg 0.5 seconds West.

Tuesday 23rd November, Atlantic Ocean

Saw 4 shooting stars last night as well as 2 other yachts whose lights we could see on either horizon running parallel to us, but it feels as though we have the ocean to ourselves again. Can't sleep tonight, got a little sunburnt on my back. 1st watch -0800hrs, just as we are finishing, we put up the spinnaker, inside out. Drop it back down and hoist it again. Back to bed. Up at 1100hrs feeling more refreshed. Our pineapples are going off now so we have to eat them quickly. I enjoy a bowl of pineapple, mango and melon under the sun, with the ocean around, life really is good. I take a Mexican shower *(bucket of sea water poured over my head)* after dropping the spinnaker, then relax in the cockpit with a lollipop- who said rock'n'roll is dead, huh? Barometer is down 3Mb since midnight, now reading 1017, could be a clue of what may lie ahead. Wind picked up a little later but still only averaging 10-15 knots, our SOG *(Speed Over Ground)* is about 6 knots which is not too bad considering. We are running a sweepstake on our ETA at English Harbour, Antigua. I've decided on 1000hrs on December 6th. Paul has chosen 2230hrs on Dec 5th. Nigel 2200hrs on Dec 5th. Let's see. We pick up 'Herb' on the VHF, and before you say anything NO-that's doesn't mean we've scored illicit substances over the radio, Herb is a weather forecaster from the USA. He broadcasts over the VHF radio to the yachting community across the Atlantic making it possible for sailors to avoid any bad weather systems before they hit, making it possible to avoid extreme winds and areas of no winds *(The Doldrums)* which can cause a vessel like ours to drift lifelessly for days or weeks at sea, not a good thing when you can't just pop to the supermarket, or you're 2,000 miles from freshwater with nothing left to drink. We eat our last fresh meal this evening, from this moment on, all we have is SOOT *(Shit Out Of Tins.)* Our position is 24 deg 55 mins .1 sec North, 20 deg 52 mins .4 seconds West. If you check the numbers, you will see we are heading further south from 27 degrees North to 24, straight towards the Low pressure predicted at 20 degrees, low pressure means no wind, no wind no progress, no progress and we could run out of food, water or diesel before we make Antigua.

Wednesday 24th November, Atlantic Ocean

 Woke this morning at 0730hrs for breakfast before putting up the Spinnaker. 0920hrs spinnaker guy line *(NOT an eyeliner for Goth Guys)* chaffed and snapped. Paul ordered all hands on deck just as the sail broke free. Mass panic to pull it in over the side before we sail over the top of it and unleash a whole world of problems. Thankfully all was well and with the aid of a little TLC, some whipping twine *(Don't go there, you naughty person)* and a 6" length of water hose *(I give up, seriously, how am I meant to work with this smut?)* , we repaired and modified the guy line just in time for lunch. Sweating like Turkey on Christmas morning, it feels bloody hot today. No time for a Mexican shower either, cleaning and maintaining the yacht took precedent. Studied some more Astral Navigation, it's starting to make sense to me now but I still have a lot to learn. Made contact with Herb tonight, advised us to stay at 23 degs North and head West, there's no wind south of 23 degrees, so we changed our heading to 270 degrees and sailed due west. Our ETA is still 5 or 6, or maybe 7 days. Our Barometer has dropped another 3 Mb today, down to 1014. Average speed since La Restinga 7knots. 428Nm behind us, 174Nm in the last 24 hours. Position 23 deg 35 min .4 seconds North, 23 deg 7 min .6 seconds West.

Thursday 25th November, out on the big wide ocean still

November? Are you sure? I'm sweating like a Broiler again, it's gloriously hot out here. Struggled to keep awake on the early watch 0400-0800hrs, Robert was hogging the helm from dawn til dusk, I may just have to disappear the next time he gets tired or the wind picks up, he doesn't seem to like being on the helm when it gets blowy. What am I bitching for? I'm still having the time of my life even if I'm galley bitch all watch long, it's better than anywhere else I could possibly be right now. Spinnaker up at 1330hrs. Practised some more Astro Nav. Wind down to 4 knots at 1335hrs. Used a lot of diesel this morning, 7.5 hours with the engine on, that's not good. Saw one of the best sunrises so far, this morning. Blue sky, tinted green, red,yellow and orange refracting off the clouds, glorious. Spinnaker up again this evening. We are being shadowed by Peter Von Seiselmerell, a German (...?) Ketch. Contacted Herb again this evening, more of the same for another couple of days, sit between 22N and 23N. Had an extra half an hour on the dogwatches this evening so that we can move the ship's clock back an hour. Midnight-midnight 175Nm Barometer 1014-1016mb. Syphoned 2 jerry cans into the main diesel tank, 40L. Our position 23 deg 17 mins .5 sec N, 25 deg 51 mins .4 seconds West.

Friday 26th November, we definitely ain't in Kansas

0000-0400hrs watch, I stole the helm by getting up early and beating Robert to the cockpit, childish but necessary for some reason. I'm smiling to myself despite the lack of wind. The spinnaker is down again and we started the engine at 0100hrs. Still being followed by the Ketch which we lose sight of at 0230hrs. Barometer steady at 1014mb. Sighted our first Dolphins for a while at 0120hrs off the port bow, last time was at Cascais, a whole lifetime behind us, their presence raises our spirits and everything feels right again. Dolphins are such magnificent creatures and out here they are the closest thing to Man's best friend. Saw a couple of squadrons of flying fish again this morning. Paul and Robert were both late to rise, they had a bad night's sleep apparently, just as I had a few days previously, whenever, wherever that was. Syphoned another 40L diesel into the tank. 2,000Nm to go still, 80L diesel used. Paul thinks we have enough fuel now for 10 hours steaming per day for 12 days, that should be more than enough. Unfortunately we are running out of kitchen roll though. Updated on Met *(meteorology, not the fuzz!)* around 1100hrs. No wind over 10 knots within 300 miles of our position with no change expected until Monday. We recalculate our diesel usage. Our burn rate is 2.3L per hour at 1900 RPM. This would give us enough until Monday plus 4 hours a day for charging our batteries plus an extra 33 hours. So long as we get some wind next week, we will be fine. More sunburn on my back today, had a Mexican shower and saw so many flying fish I couldn't even attempt to count. A cloudy evening and Martin set up a fishing line off the stern but caught nothing. Checked in with Herb who gave us a new waypoint to head for, just a little more Southwesterly to avoid a high pressure ridge, and that should then drop us nicely onto the Trade Winds. Back on deck to find we are surrounded by Dolphins, how perfect is that? I went forward and sat by the bow. There were 4 Dolphins swimming just a little more than an arm's length away from me, they were watching me watching them, these beautiful sirens of the ocean, so temptingly close to touch. 827Nm from La Restinga. Our position 22 deg 39 mins .3 seconds North, 28 deg 39 mins .7 seconds West.

Saturday 27th November, ain't in the windy city neither

 Claret and blue sunrise with mauve and purple clouds, you wouldn't believe it if you saw it in a painting, but absolutely beautiful to the naked eye. The ocean has taken on a rich blue colour that has a lovely warm feel to it, not at all like that cold to the senses blue you find on chinaware. The wind has picked up a little today. Spinnaker up at 0800hrs. Martin set out his fishing line and managed to catch a pair of lips. We are travelling too fast and the bait obviously took the face off a fish unfortunate enough to try it's luck. "All hands on deck!" Robert and Christian had just swapped over on the helm as the wind dropped and the spinnaker wrapped itself around the furling headsail. Paul rushed to the bow and Martin released the spinnaker halyard, dropping the sail to the deck. Paul unhooked the halyard from the head of the sail and then the port clew at the pole. Nigel and Christian pulled the sail in as I dived in to keep it clear of the starboard guardrail and mainsail blocks. I collected a blow from the loose clew on my shin for the efforts made, but the adrenaline numbed the pain and miraculously we managed to get the whole sail stowed without any tears to the spinnaker, no loss of the pole or any members of the crew. We were getting good at this shit, top team! It was a shame that it had happened at all, but we recovered well. A spinnaker doesn't like it when the wind drops from 15 to 9 knots in an instant, it needs a constant breeze to keep it filled out and powering the yacht. Tidied up, checked the Milk and Orange Juice stores, 16 and 8L respectively. Christian took me through his Merpass calculations and sight reductions, all clever stuff. Quiet evening tonight. 180Nm today but only 150Nm over the ground, we lost 30 Nm to drift. Our position 21 deg 04 mins .8 seconds North, 30 deg 38 mins .5 seconds West.

Sunday 28th November, between the ocean and stars

 0000-0400hrs watch. Straight into galley bitch mode, but managed to steal the helm away after Paul did a stint. Spot 'Fidelus' behind us around 0215hrs. Paul calls her on the HF radio and reports speaking to a very sexy sounding French lady from St Maarten. Slept like a log until 0745hrs. Woke up with 2 new yachts behind us. Engine off at last and a bowl of muesli mixed with orange juice. Only 15L milk left, 1 jar of coffee. We are having to ration ourselves now. Nobody's too happy with this situation but it's all we can do, there ain't no Walmart round here buddy. Spot another yacht 7 miles ahead on our bow but we lose sight of her by mid-morning. Engine is back on after lunch as the wind dies. It's bloody hot again today, too hot to be baking bread in the galley but when your skipper finds out you used to be a baker, guess what happens? The usual apres midi of sunbathing, chatting, washing decks etc. Christian appears on deck in his birthday suit, totally unfazed, unlike Paul who almost blows a gasket when he decides he's then going to top the ocean up a little more. To lighten the mood I take a tin of deodorant from my cabin and while Martin is making a brew I pull in his fishing line and tape the deodorant to it, quickly dropping back over the stern before he returns to the cockpit. "Martin, quick-I think you've caught something!" Martin races on deck, sees something bobbing around in our wake and triumphantly reels it in. It's not until he lands it on deck that the smile disappears from his face, then he grins and calls me a bastard, jokingly of course. His revenge will be thorough, of that I'm sure. Fruit cocktail and custard dessert tonight, yummy! No wind predicted until Tuesday or Wednesday, our diesel supply is running low, some other yachts in the area are already running critically low. Herb has been 100% on the ball for us so far, we will get some wind around 18 deg North. 182Nm today. Flying fish everywhere. Practiced with the sextant again today but not very successful, I couldn't get the lenses to line up in time for Merpass but managed to get a fix later on other attempts. *(Merpass or Meridian Passage, is a quick method of calculating a position line of Latitude which can be done once a day only, at noon local time, when the sun is directly overhead.)* Our position 19 deg 36 min .5 seconds North, 32 deg 44 min .2 seconds West

Monday 29th November, A breeze, a breeze, my kingdom for a breeze

 Struggled with early watch 0400-0800hrs. Emptied the last of the Jerrycans into the fuel tank, an estimated 45 hrs engine running left plus 4 hrs per day to charge the batteries, restricted the engine to 1500 rpm when in use, every drop is critical now.Sailed with 1 reef in the mainsail overnight, it made the boat handle so much better on the helm, less rolling around. Saw a pair of Fairey Terns this morning whilst looking out for Flying Fish. Very hot again today, barometer at around 1013-1015mb . Wind picked up to 12-15kn. Had the last of our part-baked bread today, I will have to make some proper bread tomorrow. 1645hrs a shoal of Tuna appeared off our stern to the starboard side, maybe 6 or 7 frantically jumping out of the water about 800m away. At first we thought they were Dolphins I didn't recognise them without their tins on. Spinnaker up again late afternoon but took it down again at sunset as the wind dropped. Pleasant warm night out on the ocean, nothing spectacular. Midnight to midnight 174Nm. Our position 18 deg 04 mins .7 seconds North, 34 deg 42 mins .9 seconds West.

<u>Tuesday 30th November, Midway across the Atlantic</u>

 Made the first of the homemade bread today. It was ok but I thought the oven may have been too hot, it could have done with another 10 minutes at gas mark 7 instead of 8, but nobody complained. Spinnaker up at 0815hrs, the wind is perfect at 19-20 knots and steady. We are steering 265 degrees now we are at 18 degrees North, very hot, absolutely lovely until lunchtime when it became hotter than hell itself. The light and heat reflecting off the yacht exacerbated the situation.Had a Mexican shower around 1400hrs, tried to sleep but it's just too hot. A spot of routine maintenance on deck, tightening down screws etc, Spinnaker still up at 1900hrs, excellent sailing and I managed to hit 10.2 Knots at one point, go team me, eat your heart out Dame Ellen, woohoo! Tuned in to Herb again tonight. We are halfway across the ocean, only 1432Nm to go. Kept the spinnaker up all night, we made 200Nm midnight to midnight. Robert doesn't want to go near the helm any more, he can't handle sailing with the spinnaker up. Paul called a meeting in the night to insist all hatches be kept shut at night as the light pollution from below was blinding our view on deck. Barometer reading 1013-1015mb. Our Position 17 deg 27 mins .1 seconds North, 37 deg 18 mins .8 seconds West.

<u>Wednesday 1st December on the home straight now</u>

 10.5 Knots over the ground, we are flying now. Couldn't sleep last night as it was too hot below deck with the hatches shut. I can't believe it's December and we're in shorts and t-shirts at night, unable to sleep because of the heat. Christian took a turn at baking our bread today. It went a little tits up as he used a ciabatta bread mix and was trying to get it to rise in the oven loaf tins. There was sticky dough growing everywhere. It ended up tasting ok but didn't look too pretty. Robert wrapped the spinnaker around the furling headsail again and Paul had to take over the helm as we fixed it. The weather has turned shitty, grey, humid and sweaty hot. It seems we may be in or around the Trough that Herb had been warning us about, we notice that the wind is turning now. Spent the afternoon cleaning. Martin approached me this afternoon and asked if I wanted to stay on board the yacht with him until January 4th. He had been employed to take over the Falcon once we arrived in Antigua and Skipper the vessel during a charter cruise for 3 passengers on a Caribbean Mile Building Cruise. I had to choose between leaving when we arrived in English Harbour along with the rest of the crew, then flying home for christmas, or staying aboard and spending Christmas in The British Virgin Isles. It was a tough one,I mean Cov or BVI's, what's a guy to do? Hell yeah, change my flight tickets and call me Captain Jack, I may not have a parrot but I can produce a pretty good wooden leg when I need to. Herb came through for us again, what an incredible guy, we are in exactly the right spot to shoot across to Antigua now. Tropical storm Ottois headed our way but we will be 360 miles away on Friday night when it arrives, but we have 25kn winds expecting tomorrow night with gusts up to 40 knots, that should be good fun. Barometer reading 1013mb, sweaty sleepless night. Our position 17 deg 01 mins .4 seconds North, 39 deg 52 mins .7 seconds West.

Thursday 2nd December, Getting closer

 Don't get me wrong, I may be a salty sea dog and love nothing more than bouncing around on the briny all day and night long, but saltwater coffee is not the best way of waking me up in the morning. Pukesville central, yuck! Someone *(Robert was very quick to blame Christian who swore it was Robert)* opened the sea water stop cock under the sink and filled the kettle with salty water. Helped Robert to bake some brown bread, the best we've had so far. Spent the afternoon on the Dog watch doing my washing and having a shave, yes we still have to keep up our appearances, can't be letting standards slip-heaven forbid. The Dogwatch *(between 1200hrs-1400hrs)* was extended again by an hour so that we are now using GMT-2 hours. Slight winds today which meant using the engine more than I would have liked, but that's just the way it is right now. I seriously want to stay in the Caribbean now but will have to see if UKSA can change my flight. Paul doesn't think the tickets are changeable, let's wait and see. Tuned in to Herb tonight but he couldn't hear us at all. There are lots of squalls ahead of us, a big low pressure area at 10 deg N 50 deg W. It could cause us some problems, 35kn winds with 10m waves, that's quite a rollercoaster. Barometer down to 1011mb. Our position 17 deg 19 mins .5 seconds North, 42 Deg 22 Mins .3 seconds West.

Friday 3rd December, Slapstick central

 Woke to the sounds of Martin calling me. I thought it was in my dream so I kept looking around wherever I was dreaming to find him, but he was calling me in the real world, asking me to help him with the bread. All was ok until the smoke alarm went off and he trapped his fingers in my cabin door, ouch! The bread was good though. 1032Nm to Antigua at 1300hrs. I accidentally threw a plate overboard with the dirty dishwater at lunchtime. I didn't know it was in the bucket until I threw it over the side, luckily we have another spare. By way of complaint the ocean is as flat as a pancake and other than me and Nigel, there's no wind, 1-2 knots if we're lucky. The Ocean is eerily flat, beautiful to look at though, even as strange as it is, I mean, this is the Atlantic Ocean but it looks like a pond on a cold spring morning. Caught a fish this afternoon but lost it pulling it in, it was a real one too, not like the Brut that Martin reeled in the other day, which he seems to have forgiven me for. We are down to around 20-25 hours of diesel left now. This is getting worrying now, we need some wind and we need it now.Herb informs us we'll get no wind until Sunday night or Monday morning, not what we wanted to hear. 153Nm midnight to Midnight, our worst day since leaving Cascais. Our position is less than ideal, but geographically 17 deg 26 mins .1 seconds North 44 degs 34 mins .3 seconds West.

Saturday 4th December, It's all happening here

 0130hrs there's a lighting storm off to our starboard quarter, really pretty to look at but I wouldn't want to be beneath it. An hour later another lightning storm off to the South. Several shooting stars but no other traffic. 5 Days now without seeing another vessel. Diesel running horribly low, no wind overnight.

Up again for coffee and weetabix before being called on deck. A Sperm whale swam along our starboard side about a boat's length away. No time to get my camera as it blew out and flipped it's tail and dived beneath us. What an incredible start to the day. A Sperm Whale 40ft away from us in the wild, people pay a lot of money to see things like this and we have ringside seats for free. As we congratulate ourselves on seeing such a beautiful creature up close, a rainbow appears in the sky ahead of us. I busy myself with the washing up and am called on deck again. Paul has spotted a Turtle off to Starboard. Robert and Nigel have decided to take 48hrs RNR in Antigua, regardless of when we actually arrive, they don't want to fly straight home without taking in some of the Island first. I suggest it a little unreasonable to expect the rest of us to clean and prep the boat they round on me like I'm the bad guy. Robert is now looking like the sort of person who's not happy unless he's blaming someone else for his bad luck, or simply bemoaning a situation. I am convinced of one thing though, if he raises his voice at me once more I will slot him once we are ashore in Antigua. Around 1600hrs the engine began to splutter. Opened the diesel tank to find about 30L left. So this is it, no diesel, no wind. Spent the evening putting the fuel tank back together and missed registering with Herb. Caught sight of Barracuda, a French Yacht. Martin called her on the HF. She's heading for St Lucia with only 48 hrs of diesel left. Kept her in our sight through the night until sunrise. Saw what I could only describe as the most fantastic shooting star I have ever seen tonight. A bright green flash blazing through the celestial sphere, dragging a huge tail behind it. The trail stayed visible for about 10 minutes after the actual sighting. It was absolutely spectacular. What a day. Our position 17 deg 13 mins .5 secs North, 46 deg29 mins .3 seconds West.

Sunday 5th December, Here it comes

Up at 1030hrs, first job to finish refitting the fuel tank sender unit, and reseal the inspection hatch. Spinnaker is up, we have 15kn of wind and are finally storming along at 9 knots, relief is not enough of a word. Picks up throughout the day, progressing to 24kn of wind and 10 knots of speed. Fantastic sailing conditions interrupted at 1400hrs by a torrential downpour, everyone soaked through to the skin, we passed around the shower gel to make the most of the free water while we can. Emptied and cleared the fridge today as it was absolutely foul. Paul gave me a pep talk on our 'wind-down', saying we had to make the most of our last 4 days or so, not to think of the end of the trip, but to enjoy but enjoy every last moment while we can. I understand him 100% this is the only time ever in my life that I will be here, in this opportunity. I can return to the sea again, but until I do, and if I don't, this is my only opportunity to make the best memories I can. This yacht, this crew, these days will never be repeated. I laid on the foredeck to dry off and contemplate my return to the UK. The agency is gone, my family split and a whole trail of tears of my own making behind me. I conclude that I must be some kind of maverick, I fit in everywhere but nowhere, but the sea loves me, I love the sea and I need to make this my life now, it's what I trained for as a kid, all those years in the Sea Cadets learning to march in time, polish my boots and master Radio Telephony, it was all tao bring me here, the seamanship, the *(sometimes lack of-)* discipline, it wasn't for nowt, it was preparation. Saw some more shooting stars tonight, couldn't sleep again. Martin showed me the Andromeda Galaxy, Orion Nebula and the 7 Sisters Cluster *(Horns of Taurus)* all clearly visible through the ship's binoculars. They're up there in the night sky, every night of our lives and yet we don't see, we don't take the time to look up and take in the incredible wonders above our heads. The unending universe beyond the petty boundaries of man.178Nm midnight to midnight. Spinnaker down at 2000hrs, too gusty to keep it up *(an excuse I've used many times since!)* Our position 17 deg 24 mins .8 seconds North, 49 deg 16 mins .8 seconds West.

Monday 6th December, Trying times

 Graveyard shift 0000-0400hrs. Spotted several excellent shooting stars tonight. The wind picked up and then died a little, but we put the spinnaker up at 0800hrs again. Robert seems to be winding me up a lot lately. Today he even snubbed Paul a turn on the helm at 0200hrs, knowing full well Paul was tired and needed to get on the helm to help wake up a bit, but then that's Robert all over, Me-me-me! *(Bitch-bitch-bitch....)* Martin tells me that Mars is visible next to Venus, I tell him it's nearer Slough and I'm sure I still have some of their chocolate in my wardrobe. I take the binoculars and scan the sky, this is becoming my new favourite hobby. Caught up with another yacht overnight, possibly the Barbaschere, but we can't be certain. All bets have been placed for our new ETA at Antigua, Thursday Night/ Friday Morning seems most likely, I've chosen Thursday 2000hrs, just in time for a nice cold Margherita. Got my head down at 1330hrs after a shower and shave, just nodded off as the call came for all hands on deck. The spinnaker halyard had given way and the whole sail was trailing in the ocean. Half awake we pulled the lot back on board and stowed it. Reset the headsail and set Martin up the mast on the Bosun's chair to recover the halyard. The ring pull on the release clip had snagged on something and sprung open dropping the kite *(spinnaker)* in mid flight. Everything was repaired and re-rigged, we raised the spinnaker again about 1700hrs, we are such a slick crew. Just getting my head down at 1800hrs when the proverbial shit hits the fan again. This time the guy rope has given way and once again the kite is taking a bath and acting like a brake on the vessel, slowing us down with the drag. Ropes are hauled, voices raised and eventually the job is done. The headsail is back up and the spinnaker is back in its bag, sulking. I caught a flying fish while all this was happening, I heard a noise by the starboard dodger and thought something else had broken. I dived onto it to stop it going back over the side just as Martin lunged with a dishcloth. The bugger stuck a spine or a tooth into my palm before being secured and then released by Christian. Excellent skies tonight, Paul was tired so we left him to sleep an extra hour or two as Robert and I chatted together in the cockpit. 178Nm today, our position 17 deg 16 mins .1 seconds North, 51 deg 56 mins .4 seconds West.

Tuesday 7th December The Good Ship Lollipop

Saw Mars and Venus rise this morning as well as the Moon occulting Jupiter, fantastic! Slept like a log through to 0800hrs, best sleep I've had in ages. Martin spoke to Fran at UKSA and doesn't think it'll be a problem to change the flights, it's looking like I'm 2nd mate to Martin for the next 3 weeks, Island hopping over the holidays. I can't tell you how excited I am because you'd only want to hunt me down and slash my tyres. Repaired another guyline this afternoon and enjoyed an excellent hour on the helm with 20kn winds, before bed again. The spinnaker is still up, but for how long? Hopefully until the morning, we have less than 450Nm to go now, the miles are finally disappearing fast. Antigua is getting closer and I'm having the time of my life. 187Nm today, our position 17 deg 09 mins .7 seconds North, 54 deg 49 mins .1 seconds West.

Wednesday 8th December So Close and yet so far

Our last full day at sea, maybe? Made good progress overnight even though the spinnaker came down. Wind gusting 24-26 knots . Woke up to a rain shower, 26kn squall and Martin on his knees cleaning up a carton of milk that had exploded on the floor. Spent a couple of hours tearing up the sole boards *(internal floor boards)* cleaning and cleansing the bilge. Took apart the salon table, cleansed under the sole, under the engine. Checked all the jubilee clips and replaced the sole boards. I baked a loaf of bread for lunch and then crunch- everything changes. The reality of everything now is setting in. It's almost over. Recipe for Sour *(puss)* Dough: Take 6 grown men, pour them into a 45ft yacht and set them loose on the ocean for 2 months. Leave to mature *(It's guaranteed they won't)* and then add an accelerant *(tell them they're only 300Nm from their destination)* and allow them to implode. 1 well honed crew will now metamorphose into 6 individual members with loose alliances to the left and right. Suddenly we have no cohesion. Nobody is wanting to talk to me, or Martin, in fact, nobody is really talking at all. And so our afternoon is spent under a bright blue sky and a big black cloud from bow to stern.I get that we all have things on our minds, home for the most part, but I don't want the entire experience sullied by a sense of melancholy, as Paul said, enjoy these moments, make them count for something, keep the memories happy for all our sakes. The atmosphere lifted a little after supper but still not right. Late shift 2000- 2400hrs was a blinder, gusting 25knots of wind with plenty of surf and corkscrewing through the waves. Robert is still not talking to me. Ended the watch clutched in Martin's arms in the galley as he slid from portside to starboard, pouring 3 mugs of hot coffee down my leg, burned my skin a little but it'll heal. We have to lift the soleboards again now, shit happens. 183 Nm midnight to midnight, 36 mugs of coffee made only 10 got drunk, the rest are sloshing about in the bilge. Our position 16 deg 54 mins .6 seconds North, 57 deg 40 mins .4 seconds West

<u>Thursday 9th December, Are we there yet?</u>

Double shift overnight, lots of shooting stars including one which lit up the mainsail again. Saw a couple of Satellites too. Took the helm at 0400hrs and refused to relinquish it other than to Paul. Payback is a bitch ,Robert. 0730hrs we dumped the mainsail and repaired the plastic clips on the sliders. Woke the opposite watch with the news that we are 170Nm from Antigua. Nigel and Robert seem to be up to something, I wouldn't be surprised if they walked off the boat once we land. Nice cup of tea and then off to bed for a bit. Woke at 1000hrs as Christian was preparing the day's bread. Martin and I get on with making an inventory of the ship's stores. We put up the spinnaker at lunchtime and have a DIY lunch. 'The Children' are in a real sulk today, I get it, they don't like that Martin and I are staying on, but that was the deal when Martin was taken on, and I am just lucky enough to have been invited to stay a bit longer onboard with him. Paul tears up the Tote envelope refusing to be held to any sort of schedule, real or invented. Had a bit of a peptalk in the cockpit but but not a word from 'The Children'- what is their problem? Got sick of it in the end when Robert made a cup of tea and then another, and another, without offering me or Paul a drink. I asked him what I had done wrong and he said he didn't want to say anything until he got back to UKSA, knowing full well I wouldn't be there. I'm getting pretty angry now and worried I might do something he'll regret, so I count to 10 and keep the toys in my pram. I sat on the foredeck for an hour alone, chilling with the sound of the ocean around me. I feel 70% better for it but decline supper this evening, I'm too tempted to pour it on his head. Made some rice pudding instead, told Robert to go make his own. 1835hrs a U-bolt snapped on a halyard at the masthead. Up went the shout, down came the spinnaker. Will need to get someone up the mast tomorrow to make a repair. No spinnaker until it's fixed. Our position 17 deg 00 mins .6 seconds North, 60 deg 34 mins .2 seconds West

<u>Friday 10th December, I can see it</u>

Graveyard shift tonight, did my best to stay polite and bit my tongue more often than I should really. I mean, I have done nothing to warrant this treatment but I sure as hell am not going to spoil my opportunity to stay aboard because of a silly old man's jealousy, if that's all it is. Bed at 0400hrs and back up at 0700hrs. Antigua is in is sight. 0800hrs and Robert is on the helm lording it, a real queen of the castle this fellow. Got on with prepping the boat until we docked. We'd run through the night with no lights on in order to preserve the charge in the batteries and the last drops of diesel to get us into the harbour. We head straight to the diesel island, refuel and refill our water tanks. Motor out to our buoy and then begin the serious work of cleaning and clearing the boat. At 1600hrs Nigel, Robert and myself head out to the airport to change our tickets. The flight to Barbados lands only 20 minutes before the London flight closes and it's decided none of us can make that connection. Nigel decides to have a week in Barbados, Robert changes his ticket to leave earlier. I changed mine to leave Antigua on 30th December. I have to return on Monday to confirm the change with British Airways as their office is closed at the moment. I am planning on arriving back in Coventry on New Years Eve. This means getting back to Antigua on the 30th or getting another flight to Barbados from any other island on the same day. We return to the Falcon and Robert departs immediately to book into a hotel and the atmosphere lifted there and then. Went out for supper and a few beers, then slept soundly the whole night long.

Cowes to English Harbour 6100Nm, 201 Night Hours, 48 days on board. Position 17 deg 03 mins North 61 deg 03 mins West.

Saturday 11th December English Harbour, Antigua

Wake up to a champagne breakfast and a lot of smiles. Everyone is relaxed and happy. Worked on the boat and despite the heat, it's hot here, very hot, we manage to get most of our work done before heading to the pub. Robert turned up and apologised for his behaviour, I hadn't seen that coming and as he was big enough to admit his guilt then I am big enough to accept the apology and forget my plan to punch him out. Got on really well with Nigel again tonight, first time for a while, I'm hoping we can stay mates now, for a while at least. I buy Paul a Lobster supper to thank him for everything, we swallow a few beers and retire for the night.

Sunday 12th December, English Harbour, Antigua

Finished the boat today. New spinnaker halyard fitted, new engine oil, re-rigged the ensign, fixed the masthead fittings and had my first real shower since Las Palmas. Martin unpacked his Saxophone and played a session in the bar before taking us all up Shirley Heights where there is a music festival taking place. The scenery above the harbour is absolutely beautiful. A slight breeze cools the hot air around us as hundreds of locals dance the night away. The music is the most infectious reggae/calypso/ska sound I have ever heard in my life. I want to go native, I never want to leave this place, the sounds, the sights, the all pervasive smell of weed everywhere. I want to say I'm in heaven, but it's better than that, so much better. Nigel and I are wasted but manage to buy a burger each from the 'Grace before Meals' shack, and it's the best burger I have ever eaten anywhere in the world, ever.

Monday 13th December, Hangover Harbour, Antigua

It's raining, it's pouring, the old man is another year older, happy birthday Martin. Cleaned everything today, popped over to the chandlers in the RIB to get some bits. Chatted with a lady called Andrea who was making a documentary about sailing with the German boat next to us. I am invited to the film premiere in Stuttgart next year. Went back to the airport to change my flight with BA. Paul, Nigel, Christian and Robert flew out leaving myself and Martin on board. The boat is cleaner and tidier than ever, and what a relief, it feels so good like having the house to yourself after the last of the raucous party people finally leave in the wee small hours and the house feels suddenly silent. I take Martin out for a birthday meal and we might even have had a beef or two. Bed at 2330hrs as there's a lot to do tomorrow.

Tuesday 14th December, Jolly Harbour, Antigua

Did our final clean down, water fill, refuel and away, just myself and Martin having some quality time on the boat. The German boat left for Guadeloupe. We slipped our berth at 1130hrs and messed about for a while between the buoys, getting used to handling the boat with only the 2 of us on board, practising our turns and tacking. Hit a squall at the entry to English Harbour and then the almost inevitable downpour of sweet, warm caribbean rain. We sail to Jolly Harbour on the headsail and engine only, we feel euphoric, it's so good to be here, right now. The water around us turns from deep blue to aqua marine, it's more beautiful than any brochure in any travel agents office. The shore is fringed with Palm trees and the sand is pure white, with green mountains and a grey sky. This is the caribbean I had come to see, this is what I was hoping to find. We docked alongside the UKSA Pelican, the sister vessel to Falcon. We take the opportunity to swap spares and repairs before going for a swim in the pool by the bar, Barbecue supper and relax, this is truly the life.

Wednesday 15th December, Jolly Harbour, Antigua.

We are joined by our new crew, a husband and wife from Brean, near Weston-Super-Mare. Steve runs a pub and his wife Beatriz is from Chile, Kevin is ex-Army and looking to become a Yachtmaster, not too different to Paul. Martin headed off to clear customs before our departure whilst the others go shopping, managing to return with cockroaches in their weetabix. None of it makes it to the boat, we bin all the cardbors and anything else that looks infested. We wash the galley with Antibac and then fit a block and tackle in order to raise the outboard motor so that we don't drop it over the stern. Once ready, we set sail just in time to get hit by the heaviest downpour since we arrived here. We head North to the beautiful little island of Barbuda. On route, we introduce the newbies to the boat, tell them where everything is, how it works and what not to do, etc etc. We arrive at Barbuda at 1700 hrs and it is truly the most paradise-like island I could ever describe. A low, white sand island surrounded by coral reefs, with narrow creeks and lush green grass and trees. We drop anchor and it takes a small part of one of my knuckles with it, ouch! We decamp the RIB and the outboard motor before relaxing for the evening. We have finally arrived in Paradise.

Thursday 16th December, Barbuda

Woke around 0730hrs, had breakfast and then spent the day swimming and walking along the beach. I don't when I died, I have no recollection, but I know I have arrived in Heaven, there is nothing that can compare to this, nothing, anywhere in the world. I find some Turtle nests on the beach, they had been raided by a cat or mongoose and many of the shells were cast aside, empty. I then found a yellow and white crab about 4" wide. He was so full of character, totally unfazed by my size and even threatened me with his pincers, he was ready to defend himself. I followed him along the bank of a creek, it was like we were dancing together just the two of us alone in the sand. I tried not to stay too long with him, I didn't want to scare, just observe. After lunch we rerigged the running gear on the foredeck and mast, dismantled the RIB and outboard, swam some more before lift anchor at 1640hrs and motored south a few miles for an early departure in the morning.

Friday 17th December St Barts

Awake at the crack of sparrow fart to the sound of my alarm clock. 0500hrs and all hands to the coffee deck. We set sail for St Barts around 0600hrs. We sent out a fishing line and caught 2 Atlantic Bonita, 3 others got away. We cut them up for lunch, bake some bread and mix some salad and dressing. Martin suggests calling me Jesus for feeding everyone with bread and fish, but I can't perfect the water to wine part of the deal and so it's a non-starter. Kevin fell asleep for most of the day after falling a bit queasy during the bakery lesson. We arrived at St Barts around 1600hrs and went ashore for ice cream,beer,

Margaritas and Pizza. It seems very expensive here, more used to the Disney cruise ship tourists that flood the place on a regular basis. Back to the boat just in time for the anchor to slip and we hit another yacht. We move to another anchorage and also put out the Kedge anchor as a back up.

Saturday 18 December, St Barts

Couldn't sleep last night, sat on the Transom having a wash at 0400hrs, felt sweaty, tired and grimey. Eventually found my form after briefing the newbies on the cockpit lockers, where everything was, what they are foe etc etc. Took a swim late morning only to notice that we'd anchored across a mooring chain. Martin devises a way to lift the anchor without snagging the mooring chain. Have another swim then measured the anchor chain, marked it lengths of 4m. Checked the engine over and found the lift pump and air intake. Had lunch, another swim and back on board. Kevin called us up on to the deck to see a Turtle swimming by. It was about 3ft long, gracious and gorgeous to see in its natural environment. Martin returned from Customs and I drove the boat while Kevin worked the anchor. Martin was in the water checking that we didn't snag the chain, reset the anchor, had another swim. Got dressed and went for a beer.

Sunday 19th December, St Maarten

Slept like a log last night and up at 0600hrs to leave St Barts and make a passage to St Maarten. Once clear of the island we sent out a fishing line, catching an Atlantic Cero that weighed in about 3lbs. Fed the line back out and immediately hooked a Little Tunny. Took the fish into the galley to prepare for lunch and baked some bread while Martin hauled in 3 more fish, including a Yellow Snapper. Finally put the rod away before we ran out of fridge space. Arrived at Gustavia, Simpson Bay Marina and had to wait an hour for the bridge to open and allow us access into the Marina. Escorted in by the Marina's RIB. Berthed nose on, with the bow against a finger pontoon. Secured ourselves with 3 bow lines, a spring line and stern line. Martin and I head to the beach in our RIB leaving the crew to do the touristy thing. Went for an evening at the Sunset Beach Bar and got totally twatted on Margaritas. Danced the night away to some great reggae and rock tunes. I love it here.

Monday 20th December, St Maarten.

Woke up this morning with the hangover from hell. Somehow I made it home last night but I'd been robbed in the process. My wallet was gone and had been replaced with a bag of green herbs. Whoever took my wallet was a dirty, sneaky bastard because I was still wearing my jeans in bed and they'd pissed all over me in my bed. I got up, washed and changed then took my bedding out and washed it thoroughly. It was late morning and I'd been left to sleep it off as the rest of the crew went ashore. Went to the beach for an hour and back to the boat. Martin filled me in on the missing bits from the night before, he told me I was funny as hell coming home, absolutely steaming and wouldn't let the taxi driver go until he swapped my wallet for a bag of herb. The mystery was solved, but who pissed on me in my bed? Martin reckoned it was Jose Cuervo, I agree, and when I find him, I will give him a proper slap. Fresh fish supper and a few beers before bed. Life is good.

Tuesday 21st December, St Maarten

Woke around 0800hrs to the sound of the 5 day weather forecast. Prepared the boat for sea and slipped our berth around 1000hrs. Once out in the open sea again we cast out a fishing line. Within minutes we pull in an Albacore, followed by a Yellow Jack and then a Spearfish. Packed the rod away and concentrated on sailing again. We headed out to Anguilla, wind 15kn and sails close hauled right up to the anchorage when we dropped sails at the very last minute, no motoring for us today. We dropped the anchor and Martin was quick to get in the water and check the chain and that the anchor took grip properly. Tidied the boat, broke out the RIB and had a swim. Did a quick repair to the mainsail halyard and filed down a burr on the pushpit. Today's loaf of bread was superb but didn't last very long, Kevin is to make the next one. Set out the Kedge anchor just to be safe. Martin went to check it had taken hold and whilst he was at the seabed, I saw something swim over where he was. It was about 5ft long and when Martin heard he was out of the water quicker than a cat on bath-day. Went ashore for an evening drink and ended up in a rum shack with the owner, Roberto. He was half blind with Glaucoma, half deaf with old age but more full of beans than many healthy folk I'd ever met. Back aboard Falcon for supper and bed.

Wednesday 22nd December, Anguilla to Tortola, BVI

Spent the day chilling and swimming. Not overly impressed with Anguilla, the bay was beautiful enough and it sounds exotic, but it lacked a certain atmosphere and hospitality. Slipped anchor at 1700hrs and took 3 hour watches to sail overnight to Tortola *(British Virgin Islands)*. Wind up to 28 knots, the sea surface a little confused with some pretty big waves. Beatriz spent most of the night screaming, she's not a natural sailor and it showed.

Thursday 23rd December, Road Town, Tortola

Landed in Road Town Village Marina around 0800hrs. Had an excellent sail overnight to get here. Cleaned up and had breakfast before an hour or two in bed. Headed off into town for some retail therapy and a Conch Roti. I cannot believe the things I'm eating out here, it's some of the most amazing food I've ever eaten and all fresh, the fish, the fruit, coconut milk, Asda will never look the same. Back to the boat for a spot of shut eye after we design a lifting cradle for the RIB. Only a week to go now and I can't believe it's almost Christmas and I'm here in the Caribbean, landing back in the UK is going to be a real cold shock to the system.

Friday 24th December, Jost Van Dyke, BVI

Did some last minute shopping including some little Virgin Isles mugs for the rest of the crew. The forward Heads is blocked again and so I pull on the marigolds and stick my hand down the toilet. Sure enough, the pipe is blocked with Baby wipes. I remind Beatriz not to flush them and it feels like I'm whistling to the wind, she doesn't get it. We head out after lunch and arrive at a bay on the little island of Jost Van Dyke, this is by far the best island we have visited, it is absolutely stunning and the colours, character and warmth of welcome are without exception. I could stay here forever. We go ashore to Foxy's nightclub/bar on the beach. I didn't know places like this existed, open air dance floor in the sand,right by the beach, lit up like a Christmas tree with more Tequila than a Mexican Taverna, I could get to like it here.

IT'S CHRIIIIISTMAAAAASSSSS!!!

Woke up around 0800hrs with a hangover, you'd think by now I would have learned my lesson when it comes to Tequila, or at least know how to avoid the morning after effects, but no, here I am banging my head on a wall wondering why the wall keeps hitting me. Washed away the aches and pains with a swim around the bay wishing all the other boat crews a happy christmas. Gave our crew their presents, which were very well received. Swam ashore and took a walk around the town. The harbour is great and the whole vibe of the place is that of a relaxed, chilled out island. It felt like real Rasta country, everyone was laid back, high and super chilled. Back to the Falcon for Christmas pudding and custard. Swam some more before going snorkelling with Martin in the next bay. Caught sight of some beautiful fish doing their own fishy things, swimming, eating, pooping and swimming some more, not too different from us really, but without the Tequila. Martin and I swam ashore, where we paid a visit to Rudy's restaurant to book a table for this evening. When we told him there'd be 5 of us he swore- "Shit man, that means I gotta go swimming again, I've only got 3 Lobsters left!" We laughed and I thought about his response, man, if having to swim out to your lobster pots is enough to spoil your day, how cool a life must you be living. I would gladly swap my life in Coventry for all of this. Happy Christmas everybody, life really is good.

Sunday 26 December, Boxing Day, Jost Van Dyke, BVI

Woke around 0800hrs and started the day by repairing a clasp around the preventer line, then damaged a hinge on the anchor locker lid. After breakfast we prepped the boat, the bay was getting busy now with other boats arriving all the time. We set sail for Virgin Gorda, Spanish Town Harbour. Martin left me to plot the headings and pilotage on arrival. This was my first time ever taking on the full role of a skipper. We passed between the Tortola and Guana Island, Grand Camanoe and Beef Island, my pilotage had to be spot on, there was not a lot of margin for error. We managed to put a line out and caught a Horse Eye Jack which we didn't eat but saved to use as bait tomorrow. Suddenly I started to receive a host of text messages from the UK. My friends and family were asking if I was OK and was I affected by the Tsunami? What Tsunami? We knew nothing about this, everything was great here. Martin checked the radio and found out that there'd been a Tsunami in Asia, a big one, hundreds if not thousands dead. Thankfully we were on the opposite side of the planet but we couldn't help but feel sorry for those affected. I didn't know it then, but later I found out that my former boss at Kentvale had in fact been caught up in the Tsunami, he was badly injured and spent months having reconstructive surgery's to his legs. Arrived safely at Spanish Town Harbour and refuelled our diesel, 60L. Moored up on a pontoon and after a shower shoreside we had a chicken supper and a few beers. Heading back to the boat I decide to take a walk instead. I had no idea where I was or where I was going. I just wanted to walk and explore. Some people will tell you how dangerous it can be to walk alone at night on the islands, or anywhere for that matter, I would agree, but I would also go with my intuition. I walked along a road for about half a mile until I came to a Rum shack, a small privately owned outlet. These are like a kiosk selling Rum and beer, sometimes legally, sometimes not, sometimes branded, sometimes moonshine. The vendors would sit nonchalantly watching TV or playing music like they were just sitting in their 'Mancave' minding their own business, the exchange of currency would be quiet, unseen and very casual, almost as if it were illegal, which it could be, maybe. I took a beer from the fridge and had a shot of fiery rum. Chatted for a few minutes and asked if there was a bar along the road. "A few miles up the road, there's a nightclub, but be careful brother!" I thanked my friend, popped the lid from my bottle and walked out into the night. I stopped at another Rum shack, and the scenario repeated itself. Eventually I came to a crossroads. As I approached I could see now the nightclub ahead on the right hand corner opposite. Between myself and the club was a gang of young men hanging around a car, somehow I had to pass these guys without getting robbed or stabbed, shot or whatever else might befall me. I kept walking without hesitation, straight towards the group. "Good evenin' Man!" One of them said. "Hi, how's it going-is the club there any good? I could do with another drink" I said offering my empty beer bottle. "Yeah it's cool Brother, you have a good Vacation dude." And without hardly a pause I passed without harm. The club was OK but there were more people outside than in. I managed to stay for one deink, then wandered off again in a different direction. I found another Rum shack and after a short pause with the patron, decided it was time to head for home I walked back along the dark empty road, back to the nightclub, waved at the group of young black guys still hanging around the car on the corner, and back along the long dark road to the harbour. I arrived back just as the sun began to rise over the horizon. Sat on the deck for a moment looking out to sea, and then finally went to bed.

Monday 27th December, Spanish Town Harbour, Virgin Gorda

Woke around 0500hrs and promptly threw up in the heads. Back to bed. Back up at 0800hrs with the squits. Back to bed until 1000hrs and time for breakfast, I feel drained, which is no surprise really. The crew had gone to visit some Baths, a natural rock pool a couple of miles away. Martin and I stayed aboard to discover lots of fibrous dirt on the engine. We will have to keep an eye on that. We refill the water tanks and prep for departure. Our next stop will be Saba. We are almost ready to go when Morgan Freeman appears on the boat next door, complete with a film crew. The boat itself is for sale and Mr Freeman looks as though he's going to buy it. Martin makes friends with a Pelican on the pontoon and takes a photo of it before we start the engine and leave. Beatriz and Steve take us out of Virgin Gorda, I do the navigation and once in deeper water we hook a fish so huge it takes our bait and all the associated tackle. We replaced the hook and bait and hauled in a Tuna only to lose it over the side before we could land it. Caught no more fish all night, only a very large clump of seaweed. We picked up a buoy by Wells Bay, Saba at 0230hrs, secured the boat and went to bed.

Tuesday 28th December, Saba

Woke up at 0700hrs to a proper view of Saba. It is a vertical rock, rising 1,000 metres above the ocean. There's no beach, no gentle slope to the water, nothing. It rises straight up from the ocean floor and is a magnificent sight to behold. We clear in with customs at Fort Bay and return to our buoy. As I ferry Beatriz and Steve to the shore, we are thrown out of the RIB by a wave just as we're about to land. Fortunately we are all close enough to get ashore and no harm is done, but Beatriz screams and is terrified by the experience. I pull the RIB onto the ramp and bail her out. I return for Martin and Kevin and we all take a walk around Saba. The road is steep, very steep and it's amazing it even exists at all, in fact it's amazing that anyone even lives here because it is so difficult to negotiate. The Dutch engineers that built the roads and town were true pioneers, masters at their art. I've walked on many mountain paths in the alps and beyond, but these are like nothing I've ever seen or experienced. Steve and Beatriz refuse to get back in the RIB and so we arrange to meet them in the harbour at Fort Bay, it's not far from where we are and it is the only way we can get them back on board now. After supper we head off for the return journey to Antigua. We sailed through the night, through winds of up to 28 knots with 2 reefs in the mainsail, and only part of the headsail unfurled. Our journey through the islands has added 600Nm to our log books, but the experience it has given will last a lifetime.

10 Union City Blues

I arrived back in Luton poorly dressed for the weather in my Caribbean best. With snow laying on the ground my sandals offer little protection. I feel awkward, I haven't worn footwear for so long that I would prefer the sting of the snow to the straps around my feet. Martin has sent some excess baggage home which I have to negotiate back to the UKSA by myself, along with my own kitbag. I make it through customs, and get a bus into London. From here it's another bus to Portsmouth and then the ferry. I arrive on the Isle Of Wight and get a taxi to the UKSA. The academy is closed for the holidays and only a receptionist is available, I leave Martin's baggage with her and walk out to my car. It's still there, on the slope in the car park. The batteries are all but dead but by rolling downhill the engine starts for the first time and I sigh with relief. It's a short hop through the narrow streets to the chain ferry. Another short drive to the main ferry terminal in Cowes and the crossing to Portsmouth. I've docked here so many times over the years on my journeys home from Europe, but this time it feels different, I feel like a stranger. I don't feel attached to anything here, it's all alien to me. I drive home to Coventry, just in time to dump my bag, have a shower and head off to The Jailhouse. I wear a bright blue silk Hawaiian shirt I bought in Road Town. I don't care how cold it is outside. I don't care how odd I look to the punks in the Jailhouse. I don't care who is playing tonight. I don't care about anything, I just want to get drunk and dance.….

ABOUT THE AUTHOR

Since releasing My Sequel-Innit? Wayne Reid has contributed to Eighth Day Magazine and written lyrics for Costa Rica based Gothic Rock band Last Dusk, appeared as a Guest Author for the Rock'n'Roll Book Club in London and appeared on Brazil's GloboTV as well as becoming Director of Secret Sin Records Ltd, home of Gothic Rock legends Angels Of Liberty. Currently residing with his wife Laurel Reid in Sudbury, Suffolk, UK. The pair are planning to relocate to the USA in the near future.

Printed in Great Britain
by Amazon

32902263R00086